Windows To The Soul

J. M. Barlog

BAK
BOOKS
Wheaton, Illinois

WINDOWS TO THE SOUL

Published by BAK Books

For information address: BAK Books

ISBN 0-9654716-6-7

BAK Books are published by BAK Books, a division of BAK Entertainment, Inc. Its trademark, consisting of the words "BAK Books" is Registered in U.S. Patent and Trademark Office. BAK Books, P.O. Box 94, Wheaton, Illinois 60189-0094

Printed in the United States of America
OPM 0 9 8 7 6 5 4 3 2 1

To Mary

Special thanks to James N. Doty for his diligent editing, astute suggestions and a patient willingness to read and reread and reread in order to bring this book to life.

Prologue

Ranhurst College, August 27ᵗʰ. Althea Goodfellow returned for her junior year lugging suitcases crammed with hopes and dreams. In previous years, this was a time of apprehension and the emptiness that comes with separation. But this year she arrived filled with anticipation and an undercurrent of excitement.

She marched with determination down the corridor of the Pendleton Courts dorm against the squeak of running shoes over freshly waxed floors. When she stopped at her door, the silence caved in around her. Ali had returned on the Friday *before* move-in weekend; and as such, she became the first to take up residence in the twenty-room, barracks-type structure. For all its shortcomings, (no air conditioning and communal bathrooms) Camp Pendleton as the kids tagged it, was home. This became the place where she spent three quarters of her year. Indiana had been relegated to her summer home.

A concentrated paint odor assaulted her nose the moment she pushed open the door. Ali banged the window frames to break the paint seal binding them shut, then opened them full tilt and switched her box fan on to high before taking up the task of lining her nest with those things that make the place feel more like home. *Wasted time is gone forever.* Posters of Speedo-clad beef cakes shared the walls with marquee posters of Schwarzenegger and Gibson. She then checked for dial tone, filled her closet and drawers, arranged her desk, then made her bed before stretching out on it.

The telephone's ring awakened her two hours later, and Ali snatched it off its cradle trying to keep her budding excitement out of her voice. He said he would call and he did.

"Hi, sure, Chandler. Yeah. Nine? Why can't we... No, that's okay. See you then."

After hanging up, Ali two-stepped across the room to the spell of a country ballad playing inside her head.

Sinuous, petite, and beautiful all described Ali. But the one word people associated most with her was fast. Althea Goodfellow *owned* the record at Ranhurst for the four hundred meters. Not something many people knew, but a distinction all her own nonetheless. Someday, and she told this only to herself, she would dig her toes in at the start line of the Olympics.

Three hours later, armed with a backpack slung over her shoulder, Ali closed her windows, slipped her favorite tape into her yellow sports Walkman and left her room.

Against the listless rays of a dying ocher sun painting an ivy-infested, weathered old building in a secluded corner of the Ranhurst campus, Ali waited.

She played the dim light off her watch.

Nine-twenty. He was late.

Sawyer Brown's 'The Race is On' began, soothing a tremor rumbling beneath the surface. A small round light growing on the walkway snared her interest.

Then an icy hand took her shoulder.

"It's about ti..."

A pungent cloth smothered her words, caught her windless. Ali needed desperately to draw in air. Her scream died within a fiery throat while ripping hands clawed her flesh and wrestled her from the walkway. Tears stole her vision. Helpless, Ali focused on the now crystallizing round light, praying for it to rescue her.

Then all went black.

****

In a place no longer in the world of the living, flickering candles cast a pallid glow upon a charcoal pentagram etched into a crude oaken slab. A drop of ruby blood splashes to desecrate a symbol of fornication in the pentagram's core, while Bloodstones glisten in each of four of the five points.

The fifth point remains empty.

An ancient stone deeply-rooted in man's belief system, one man had found a way to unleash its diabolic powers—to bridge a previously impassable chasm between worlds. Before he died, he recorded what he had learned.

Twenty years later someone had found his writings. Someone new now had the power to unlock what had been hidden away for centuries.

"*Asmodeus, erus meum animus esse tuus.*"

Sacred words. Words that traverse a black void that separates worlds.

Hands, smooth and uncalloused, elevate one of the Bloodstones from its place on the slab. For a moment the flickering light catches the stone's brilliance. Then this amulet comes to rest suspended around a robed neck. A face hidden by a cowl contorts into a vicious rictus as thick saliva drools from curled back lips to expose the glistening teeth of something no longer of this world.

"*Asmodeus, erus meum animus esse tuus.*"

The time for Asmodeus draws near.

1

School Daze

"You *think* your roommate's missing?" he said with an irritating ring of condescension.

My head throbbed from the jabbing din of a hundred ongoing conversations, ninety-six degree heat and the gray cloud of cigarette smoke slushing back and forth overhead. I stood before a rock-shouldered, ill–tempered prodigious black member of the Ranhurst police force. Well, they're not really police. Public Safety officers, actually. The big difference is these guys can't carry guns. And the student body here at Ranhurst thanks God for that. TANNER, his badge read. And I detected only the culmination of day-long frustration in those dark apathetic eyes.

I repeated what I had just said over the clamor of a couple hundred students crammed into the small basement lobby all trying to register their cars on campus.

"I'm serious. My roommate may be missing," I insisted when Tanner looked beyond me to the others still in line. My brewing anger buoyed to the surface.

He shifted in his crumpled and sweat-stained uniform as if to indicate that he had had a long and difficult day and no longer wished to be bothered by some spoiled, sniveling kid.

"If a student doesn't show up for college, it's none of our business. And, if a girl decides to spend the night in other than her room, we frankly don't care. You understand what I'm saying?"

I unleashed a fury that had been bottled up inside all day. This place was like a pressure cooker. I needed to get away from the stinking smoke.

"Now look, Ali moved her stuff in four days ago. I haven't seen her. Nobody's seen her. You understand what *I'm* saying?"

"Then you saw her at Ranhurst this past weekend?"

"Hel–lo. No! I haven't seen her at all. Is there a bulb burned out in there?"

"Watch yourself, young lady," Tanner shot back with a leveled finger. "Take it to the watch commander," he added with a tone of finality, indicating a barrel-shaped man wearing a laughable silver-gray toupee and immersed in paperwork behind a metal desk. I think the watch commander must have overheard our exchange, because now he forced his eyes to remain on his work and refused to bring them up to meet mine.

I swallowed my frustration long enough to repeat my story to the ambivalent watch commander, who seemed to think everything could be made better if he just smiled and said, 'I understand.' An attitude seems to permeate the faculty and staff that even though we're adults, we're still to be addressed like children.

Amazingly, I held my tongue in check—which is a difficult thing for me to do—hoping control might at least keep these people from tuning me out. My irritation, however, crept back into my voice.

"What do you expect from us?" he responded when I had no more story forthcoming.

My face turned ruddy with erupting rage. I wanted to reach over the desk, grab him by the shirt collar and shake him until his brain snapped back into its socket and began working again. Instead, I tightened my fist and counted inside my head. By ten I felt in control again. My jaw muscle slackened and I could start again, hoping this time something might get through.

However, during our less than cordial exchange, a soft-bellied, retirement-age captain with sparse graying hair and a face with a bulldog's jowls, emerged from a windowed office in the corner. His gray eyes offered concern.

"I'm Captain Merrifield. Can I help?" he injected with a voice as soft and reassuring as my father's, in an attempt more to spare his watch commander than to assist me.

"Hallelujah! I hope somebody can. I'm trying to tell *someone* my roommate is missing."

"And your name is?"

"Trish. Patricia Van Worten. Ali Goodfellow moved her stuff in over the weekend, but nobody's seen her. It's been four days."

Using a stubby finger with most of the nail picked away, Merrifield motioned me away from the commotion. I watched relief wash over the watch commander's face. He returned to his paperwork as if nothing of any consequence had transpired. How could nobody care?

"The first week back is usually very trying. It's not unusual for kids to wander in late," Merrifield said in his smooth paternal voice, once we had escaped the discord. He must have hoped his restraint would become infectious.

Inside I was still fuming. But I figured if I mimicked him, I might get through that lead skull and reach his brain.

"I know Ali, she wouldn't take off."

"You think she might have taken off?"

I locked on Merrifield's eyes. He made no effort to hide the sympathetic indifference in those gray orbs. Even after my explanation, Merrifield remained aloof and unaffected.

"Maybe Ali, what's her last name?"

"Goodfellow."

"Althea Goodfellow," he paused while he contemplated the name. "Track team. She set a school record in the four hundred meters. I ran in college, though you'd never know it now."

"She'd never be late. I know her well enough after rooming with her two years to know there's something wrong!"

What could I say to get this Merrifield guy to listen to me? You don't move everything important to you into your room and then take off. Besides, kids with problems take off. Kids who have it cozy in the nest just don't fly away.

"I understand, I really do. But this happens all the time. I'd be willing to bet she shows up in the next day or so, and all is forgotten," he said trying to consummate this without a need to initiate action. From his girth, I would think action would the last thing on his agenda.

"You're not going to do anything, are you? No one's seen her in four days, and you're not going to do anything."

"What would you have us do? We don't even know if she's lost. Have you talked with the girl's parents?"

"No."

"Then I suggest you start there. If they believe their daughter is missing, *they* should contact this office. We'll take it from there."

"Then, Captain Merrifield, I'd expect a call."

"Miss Van Worten, students are free to come and go as they please. We don't do bed checks. If you get my meaning."

I left Merrifield standing with a smug glimpse of a smile on his face as I stammered back into the crowd. I had nothing else to say.

2

What's In A Name?

Sitting crossed-legged on my bed with phone to my ear, I scrambled to line up ways to mask the concern likely to spill over into my voice. How do you start a conversation like this? Finally I realized there was just no gentle way to handle it. After the third ring I ran out of time. A timorous voice answered.

"Hello, Beth. Trish Van Worten."

After her divorce three years ago, Ali's mother insisted Ali's friends call her Beth, said it made her feel younger. I felt uncomfortable trying to think of Beth as anything other than Ali's mom.

6

The leaden pause left me fumbling. My rehearsed lines turned to vapor. The more I stumbled, the worse it would seem.

"What's the matter?" Beth asked, suddenly alarmed.

Silence proved more profound than words.

"It's Ali."

"She's okay, isn't she? She hasn't had an accident?"

I braced myself for rough going.

"Ali's not here. She's, um...I haven't seen her. I've been here since Saturday."

This was Wednesday. Ali never skipped classes.

"You haven't seen her? Her father was supposed to drop her off on Friday."

"Beth, Ali was here. Her things are unpacked, and she's all ready for class."

I scanned her clothes in the closet and the snapshots Ali had taped up around the common mirror. She had every intention of being here. That's what was scaring the hell out of me.

"I don't understand," Beth said. Fear rocketed to the top of her voice. A fear escalating rapidly toward outright panic.

"I don't either. When I talked to Ali two weeks ago, she told me she'd be in on Sunday. I was surprised to see her things already moved in on Saturday."

"She told you Sunday? She told me she had to be there Friday for track or something."

I worked the phone cord through trembling fingers while my heart pounded out chaotic thumps. Sunday? Friday?

"I just came from the practice track. Coach Benji said he had told his runners he would not be available until Tuesday." I had to focus. My mind kept slipping into thoughts of dread.

Silence flooded the line between us.

"You're certain Ali said it was for track?" I asked finally.

"I think...I don't know. Somebody called her the first week of August. About four weeks ago. A few days later she said she had to be at school early. I didn't want to take off work to drive her, so her father drove her on his way to D.C."

A sickening still choked off the line. Moments passed. Neither of us spoke. I was thinking, she was worrying.

"Ali wouldn't do anything crazy, would she?" Beth asked, wrestling with a mother's doubt about her own daughter. The two kept no secrets from each other, at least that is what Ali had said once. Ali always confided in her. But maybe some secrets a child never discloses—even to parents.

"Ali's a straight arrow. That's why I called. I'm worried."

"Let me reach her father. Maybe she went with him to that publishing convention. It would be just like her to take off without telling anyone. I'll call later. You hear anything, call back collect, okay?"

I cradled the phone but held it, hoping it would ring. Hoping it was Ali calling to say she was on her way and would be there in an hour. Finally, I let the phone go but clung to the hope that Ali would call.

Rhonda rapped once, then stuck her head in. Concern lined her impish face framed in jet black curls. Her usual perky smile was absent. Her eyes searched mine.

"Anything?"

"Nothing."

"What do you think happened? You think she went home?"

"Just got off the phone with her mother. Ali didn't go home. She hasn't talked to her mother."

"Strange. But let's not worry. Ali's okay. She'll be here. Charlie's, say ten-*ish*?"

"Can't. Fifty pounds of reading…and I want to be here if Ali calls."

Three days into the fall semester and already I am buried in class work and facing a monster quiz in Algebra. Why did I want to come back to this?

Rhonda struggled to offer a brave smile, one of genuine concern rather than a negative account balance. You see, Rhonda served as the dorm's banker. Her attorney father—divorced and shacked up with a woman the same age as his daughter—gave her a monthly stipend of three hundred dollars, which Rhonda loaded out at a modest interest (guilt money, I suppose. You leave your wife of twenty-seven years for a teeny-bopper and you need to do something to win back your daughter.) We could always count on Rhonda to help us through when our allowance was late. Mine was habitually late. I still owed Rhonda from last semester. Did Ali owe her also? I wondered for a brief moment while Rhonda closed the door.

I had returned to Ranhurst expecting a tough junior year. But I never expected this. I paced, ruminating over what I had gleaned. Ali doles out one story to me, another to her mother. Coach Benji said he would *not* be available until

Tuesday. But did he tell the entire team, or everyone except Ali? Could Ali have come back early to meet Benji? Had the coach gotten *too* close to his star athlete? Benji's a touchy, feely kind of coach. He likes putting his arms around 'his girls.' The thoughts swirled inside my head. But Benji was *too* short, *too* round, and though pleasant, anything but attractive to a young woman looking to explore the uncharted territory of her budding sexuality.

Minutes later I dismissed it. I walked over to the snapshots on the wall and stared at one of Ali in a bikini sprawled on the beach. I always ended up comparing myself to her. She had the body I wish I had. Not that mine's so bad. It just lacked those healthy endowments that men find so desirable. I counted my willowy blonde hair at the top of my list of accouterments, though Ali, whose boyish chestnut brown lacked seductive allure, seemed to attract guys like a love magnet. Ali's smile alone proved irresistible, her body consummate, and she could win over any man on campus given an hour's time. Benji, on the other hand, fit a list of nondescript adjectives as long as his arm. Well, his arms weren't really that long. A complete mismatch. Besides, Ali liked flashy guys, guys who set her on a pedestal and pump out real bucks to show her a good time.

Beyond my room, the cacophony of blasting stereos chipped away at my tenuous concentration. I had to focus. I opened Sociology. I stopped after a few pages. Whatever I had just read slipped away like water through a sieve. How could I concentrate knowing something was wrong?

Why tell me she was coming in on Sunday when she knew she would arrive Friday? Just for a few more inches of closet space? She always took some of my space anyway, and I never complained. Okay, I didn't complain too loudly. Well wait, I did snap last year and carried around that chip for the first week of classes. It was stupid. I didn't own enough clothes to fill my side.

I abandoned my book—studying became useless. I crossed to Ali's desk, not at all certain what I wanted to find. This girl kept everything so neat. Nothing scattered about, nothing to clutter things up. First week of class and my desk could qualify for disaster relief.

Something somewhere, I thought, might offer up a clue to what happened. I began in the wide desk drawer. What I sought, I had no idea. Maybe Ali left behind something to indicate where she went. Her drawer warehoused pens, old papers, a handful of tea bags and instant soup mix, cough drops, aspirins, and Band-Aids. A half dozen cassette tapes—all country— that was Ali. I recognized Eddie Rabbitt. His music was so-so, but I could sure get used to waking up to that face. I picked up another, staring at the group on the insert, Sawyer Brown, then slid it back into the drawer. The name sounded familiar; Ali must have raved about them last year.

I flicked aside Highlighter pens to get at Ali's address book. Pages of names. Friends from back home in Indiana and at Ranhurst. I wondered how many Ranhurst names had returned.

A notepad snared my attention. Did she write anything down? I brushed my fingertips lightly over the top sheet looking for impressions left by a writing instrument. *Smooth.* I stared for a long time at a frayed spiral notebook crammed with caricatures. Ali doodled incessantly when bored. She had a peculiar talent for transforming names into caricatures. Most of the names became notches representing guys she had dated over the past two years. White space was scarce. Ali liked men almost as much as she like winning. I studied the scribbles, hoping for inspiration. I got zip.

Failing to extract anything useful, I returned the notebook and other papers to the drawer. The side drawers held old cards, photographs and opened letters. I stared at a couple of group shots containing Ali. This girl saved everything. Yet she maintained it all in neat compartments. She kept her life as orderly as her desk. That made her disappearance all the more alarming. She would have left a note, or at least called somebody by now to let them know she was on her way.

My search turned up nothing. Did Ali meet someone? Did she talk to anyone?

Adrift in my thoughts, and forced to consider the worst, I sat on my bed and stared vacantly at my desk. Sociology stared back. So did Algebra. I really wanted to study; I needed to break the inertia of summer vacation and force myself back into the habit of struggling through chapters of dry text and unending strings of indecipherable mathematical hieroglyphics.

But Ali consumed my mind so totally that all else fled. At 9:30 I picked up the phone, dialed Beth's number. Busy. Beth could be yelling at Ali right now, laying in to her for taking off for

D.C. without telling anyone. Ali would blame me. But she'll get over it.

A knock drew me from the busy signal.

Colin eased open the door, his lanky six foot frame filling the doorway. That head of straw-colored hair had been bleached by the California sun and stood up as if charged with static electricity. He wore rainbow-colored jams and a shirt so bright you needed sunglasses just to look at him. We must have seemed an odd match together, he being so tall to my five foot three, even though we weren't *really* together. He kept pursuing, and I kept evading. We both knew too well what he wanted.

Behind him a studious, earthy face followed. The deep hazel eyes gazed about like a lost soul adrift in rough waters. When those innocent teddy bear eyes caught mine, they refused to let go. I smiled. He smiled back. His thatchy, rust-colored hair seemed fashionably in line with his oversized drab-colored clothes, but definitely out of step with the nineties campus scene.

"How was your summer, Colin?" I said.

"Hey, pretty great. Did some surfing, had a bitchin' time on the beach."

I envy any kid who can take summers off. I worked my ass off, and I still came up short for this year's tuition.

"Meet my new roomie. He's a Brit. His name is Quentl...bee Clang..."

"Quenby Clangston," the studious one injected to squash Colin's imminent failure.

Boy, can Colin mangle a name.

"Quenby, you're not from around here?" I asked.

"How could ya'll tell?" Quenby said, molding his voice into a terrible Texas rendition. His innocent smile had a way of latching on to you. I liked him immediately.

Quenby slid into the chair at Ali's desk while Colin took mine, and I shifted over to my bed.

"Quenby's here for a year. Then it's pip-pip, cheerio, and back to merry old England."

"What do you think so far, Quenby?"

"Only been here a week. I haven't met many people, but for right now, it's how you Yanks say, really swell!"

"Really swell? Colin, get him signed up for English 101 on the double."

"I do think I'm going to like it here," Quenby said. His eyes never left mine. He tried to mask his interest, but I could still see it in the way he looked at me.

Missy poked her head in. Her room was across the hall from mine. That meant somewhere in college dorm etiquette that we had to be friends.

"I take it nothing from Ali?" Missy asked me, all the while browsing over Quenby.

"Trish's roommate hasn't been seen since last Friday," Colin explained for Quenby's benefit.

"Maybe it's a last fling, as you Americans say, before trudging back to school. She'll show straight away."

I dismissed Quenby's remark even before he finished it.

Missy invited herself in and posted herself next to Quenby.

"You sound British. Are you British, Quenby?" Missy asked, her smile obvious. She

began primly twirling her hair through her
fingers. There was the sign again. Missy was
interested in Quenby. That must be the way they
flirt in Kentucky.

"What doesn't make sense..." I started.

"Hold on, Trish. I know what you're thinking.
Ali's probably just shacked up with some summer beau." Colin astutely deciphered the rising
glint in my eye.

"I don't think so. Ali tells me two weeks ago
she'll be in on Sunday, but prior to that conversation she told her mother she had to be on
campus Friday."

"So?"

"So the chronology's all wrong. Why lie to
me? Why not say she's coming in on Friday? Her
mother said someone called her, wanted her
back early."

"*'But prior to our conversation, the chronology's all wrong,'* Trish, you're turning this into
one of your FBI things, aren't you?" Colin said.

"FBI thing?" Quenby asked, raising a smile.

"Oh yes, Trish wants to be a G-man," Missy
shot in.

"Just because you want to join the FBI
doesn't mean you have to make a federal case
out of everything that happens. Just leave it
alone, that's what they pay the cops for," Colin
said, a little too loudly."

"You want to be in the FBI?" Quenby commented. His eyes were stuck to mine. Missy's
eyes were locked on Quenby.

"I hope to...if I can get through college."

"That's great. What is it? Sounds impressive.
Is that your secret agents or something?"

"Federal Bureau of Investigation. They handle the *big* stuff."

"Like Miami Vice?"

"No. Bigger," I said sharply, hoping to short circuit the conversation.

"Like to shoot guns, ah?"

Quenby stopped suddenly; his ramblings were making light of what could be a serious situation. I could see concern in his eyes despite the way he kept looking me over. When I glanced at Missy, she shot me a look.

Like it's my fault this Brit seems interested in me.

"I'm telling you Ali's missing. There's something wrong."

"I understand how you feel. She'll turn up. Don't let a *Top Cops* mentality get the better of this," Colin said.

"I'm concerned, okay."

"Hey, anyway, you going out tonight?" Colin asked, steering out of rough waters. "Phi Delta Phi's throwing a bacchanal. Party Meister got us on the list."

"I'll go," Missy shot in. Neither Colin nor Quenby acknowledged her.

"I'm staying here. And Party Meister, try not to retch up your guts. I won't be there to pull the bottle from your hand."

"I guess that's your job now, old chap," Colin said to Quenby, faking a British accent.

They left Missy standing in my room. Had I agreed to go, they would have had to let Missy tag along. And Missy knew it.

"Thank you heaps and noodles," was all Missy said before departing.

****

By eleven, quiet settled in over the dorm, except for the occasional barb of raucous laughter. I forced myself through the first Sociology chapter. Then I shifted to Algebra and tackled some equations meant to refresh rusty minds. Polynomials—I hate those vile little rascals, whose sole purpose is to confound, confuse and destroy. I accept that I'll never be a mathematician. Who would want to be anyway? I just needed to pass one stinking math class to complete my degree requirements. I might need a miracle to get it. Then I decided to save that miracle. I might need it for something more important.

At last the telephone rang, ending the dragging hours of uncertainty. I jumped off the bed and snatched up the phone as if it had all been an elusive dream.

"It's about time," I scolded anxiously.

"It's Beth. You hear anything?"

"Nothing."

"I finally reached Ali's father. He's leaving D.C. tomorrow; he'll be on the road for the next two days. He says he dropped Ali off Friday morning, moved some boxes around, then left."

"Did Ali say where she might be going?"

"No."

"Did Ali say who she spoke with on the phone?"

"She mentioned a name, but I don't remember it."

"Was it Coach Benji?"

"No, I'm sure it wasn't. She never said the coach had called. It was somebody else... Mike...no."

"Hold on a second, Beth."

I tossed the phone to my mattress while I retrieved Ali's directory. My hands began to sweat, my throat turned to parchment. My mind raced in a thousand different directions.

"You're certain it was a guy's name?" I pressed upon returning.

"Not absolutely certain. It had an M sound. Mark maybe?"

I flipped pages.

"No Marks, what else? This could be important."

"I'm sorry, I just can't think of it."

I detected that Beth was slowly abandoning control. Each moment of uncertainty gnawed away at her. I knew I had to hurry if I hoped to get anything of value. We desperately needed a starting point. A place to begin assembling the bits and pieces of Ali's life from the time she arrived at Ranhurst to the present.

"What about Murray?"

"I don't think so. It's a short name."

Silence cluttered the air. One syllable.

"Beth, you have to call campus security."

"Already did. The moment I hung up with Ali's father."

"What did they say?"

"The duty officer suggested I contact friends, relatives and acquaintances to make she didn't just go off on a whim. Trish, I know she wouldn't do that."

I heard little while I thumbed back and forth through directory pages, frantic to lock on to any M sounding name.

"Mary, Mickey, Marty. You're sure it was a guy's name?"

"I think so."

"Did Ali talk about track?"

"I didn't really hear much beyond Ali greeting the caller by name. Trish, Ali wasn't upset or angry about anything. We had a good summer. We disagreed at times, but she would never have taken off. I know that."

"I know, Beth. Ali had dreams and goals for this year. She wouldn't take off. She had everything going for her."

"I'm leaving early tomorrow. I can't stay here. I'll be on campus by evening. Will you wait up for me?"

"Absolutely, and I'm going back to Public Safety first thing in the morning to hound them into taking action."

I hung up without a good-bye and laid on my bed, clutching Ali's address book. My mind conjured visions. Visions that struck terror in me. Would they discover Ali's body in the neighboring woods? I shuddered, fighting down an urge to scream.

The thought also forced me off the bed. Movement stimulated thought. My pacing stretched from end to end in the twelve-by-sixteen room like a caged animal. Somebody called Ali. Somebody wanted her on campus Friday. Why? And who?

Lost in a labyrinth of jumbled thoughts, I stopped at the closet. What was Ali wearing the day she disappeared? That drew me to Ali's clothes. Did she pack a bag? Most everyone on campus used some sort of backpack to lug books around. Ali's was missing. I tried to organize an inventory, picking through the hangers. Ali had her favorites. Were they gone? When I reached the last hanger, I dislodged a pair of faded Guess jeans hung on a hook.

What's missing? I couldn't know. Could Ali have taken off? I couldn't know.

When I grabbed the jeans to return them, I felt something round and hard in a front pocket. I removed an egg-shaped stone, about twice the size of a kidney bean. A gilt wire cage trapped the strange stone inside as it dangled from a piceous woven necklace. The continuous loop slid smoothly through my fingers. No clasp, no knot. Upon closer scrutiny, I determined that the necklace had been made from finely interwoven strands. I had never seen anything like it.

Guilt marched into my head—I was invading Ali's privacy—yet I returned the jeans to the hook and carried the stone to my desk for a more intense examination. I palmed the gem under the harsh white light from my study lamp. Beneath the murky surface three diamond-shaped specks threw off the blaring light in all directions. The piece held me spellbound. In a double helix spiral, jasper veins worked their way through the stone's essence. The more I saw in the stone, the more intrigued I became with it. It seemed more like something someone would acquire at a flea market or craft bazaar rather than a jewelry shop.

The longer I stared, the more the stone crawled inside me. So much so, that I slipped it over my head, where it came to rest in the soft fold between my breasts, directly over my heart. Too low, I thought, rubbing a finger over the curve. Going to the mirror, I elevated it to just below my neckline. That felt odd for a reason I can't explain, so I released it. Wearing it sent a warm, sweet rush through me. I began to tingle; it made me sort of giddy. A feeling that had been absent in my life since early childhood.

I returned to my search. *M calls Ali.* I opened full drawers, searched the clothes carefully, then closed the drawers. *So if Ali had decided to take off, why leave all this behind?* Most had designer labels. And it wasn't that she came from money. Her parents were no better off than mine, struggling to get me through college. But Ali's free ride at Ranhurst relieved her parents of the tuition burden. Hence, Ali had money to spend on nice clothes and other amenities. Mine had to rely on grants and loans to keep me here, which my father reminded me of during his *'you-better-do-better-this-year'* speech before saying our good-byes at the car. How can I do better when I can't get my mind off of Ali's disappearance?

Nothing yet sparked my memory. But I refused to give up. I locked a tight fist around the hope that something here might trigger a clue. How come it's always so easy on television? Maybe because this is real life! And in real life bad things happen to good people. And dead is really dead.

Back at the closet, a seductively sheer azure blouse with faint winged doves ignited something inside. *Why?* I removed it, held it up against my chest while looking at it in the mirror.

"I hate girls with perfect bodies."

The blouse was one of Ali's man teasers. Who could resist her bust in this? On her, it was just tight enough to make every male head turn. My eyes worked up from the blouse to my face.

I stopped suddenly, sucking in a breath.

Something...was there...in the reflection of my eyes.

I edged closer, moved to within inches of the glass. Behind those reflected blue eyes—my eyes—I picked out something green...I moved closer. Vertical slits stared back at me.

My gasp caused the slits to vanish. An icy shiver swam through me.

The telephone's ring brought a scream. I dropped the blouse and retreated from the mirror, but I had to turn back—had to check myself once more. Maybe the stress of worrying about Ali was getting to me.

Rhonda called with a bottle of Southern Comfort and an invitation. Seems her beau had a friend dying to meet me. Yeah right. Even though alcohol was taboo in the dorms, most of us had clever ways of sneaking it in without the resident advisors detecting it. Besides, getting caught rarely brought anything more than a slap on the wrist and the booze being confiscated, which meant it would be consumed by the resident advisers.

I heard little, but declined anyway, the entire time staring at my reflection.

"Matt!" I chimed a second later.

"Girl, what on earth are you talking about?"

The crumpled blouse.

"Rhonda, I gotta go. Call you later."

Ali had worn *that* blouse the night she met Matt. She had said the blouse had worked again. But Matt who?

I snatched up Ali's personal directory and flipped pages. No Matt. But that was right. They dated briefly in the spring, then broke up. In anger, Ali had sliced up anything with his name on it.

I dialed.

"Beth, the caller's name was Matt," I said with excitement in my breathing. It wasn't a query. I was certain I was right. I could feel my heart hammering against my chest. We had our first bit of useful information.

"Matt. It could have been. I'm just not completely sure. No, you're right, it was Matt. Matt who?"

Beth's voice bubbled. We knew who; we still needed a why.

"I don't know. I can't remember his last name. And it's not in Ali's book."

I hung up. Find Matt's last name. I struggled with the blank spots in my memory. School forced me to clutter my mind with far too much academic trivia. This was important. Polynomials paled in comparison. Matt. A junior like Ali. In a fraternity...maybe. I fumbled with my recollections. He had a last name. Why did it escape me now?

The Ranhurst directory! Fifty-six pages of minuscule print listing the more than 7,000 student names, addresses and telephone numbers. And, of course, the names were in order by last name. I grabbed a pencil determined to uncover Matt's last name, even if I had to search every page to do it.

The thrill of unearthing something pertinent, along with my exhaustion, drew me into a dreamless sleep.

3

Seeing Is Believing

I left Algebra class shelving a mountain of totally foreign verbose explanations. After four days, I realized this was going to be one tough semester. When does it get easier? I asked myself as I wormed through the crowded walk.

Missy exited the Physical Sciences building and called to me as she descended the steps. A Kentucky Baptist born and bred, Missy was quiet, demure and still a virgin. I'm serious. Of course, that could be because she's still waiting to outgrow her baby fat and acne. Most poked fun at her. At times I felt sorry for her. She's nice and everything, but she can get on your nerves.

People need faults to make them human. Missy refused to accept that she had any. It was approaching noon, so we headed for the Pendleton Courts cafeteria.

A scorching sun perched itself atop a cloudless sky while below students sought refuge beneath a dappled canopy on a grassy knoll across from Administration. Shade provided the only relief from the relentless heat, unless you were lucky enough to have an air conditioned dorm room. I watched as a guy I placed in his late twenties with shaggy, uncombed hair and dressed right out of Woodstock rose head and shoulders above the onlookers, then hoisted a leather-bound Bible as if it were a monolith that all must fall to their knees before.

His sonorous voice bellowed with the chime of great cathedral bells. His words carried not only with gravity but distance as students clear across the commons turned in the direction of the grassy knoll.

"Praise the Lord, Jesus Christ loves you..." his passionate cry began over the din of mostly disinterested students.

Before he could start anew, raucous laughter and heckles crowded him out.

Though only a few years older than those around him, his dress and manner came right out of an old dog-eared sixties photograph. It was as if he were some kind of time traveler.

Missy stopped to listen.

I gently applied guidance to ease her on her way.

"Lunch, remember?" I said.

"Come on. We've got a minute."

"I'm hungry. Besides, we already have a resident lawn preacher. What's this guy trying to do, muscle in on Peter's whatever you call it."

"Following."

"What?"

"Peter's following. Doesn't hurt to listen."

"Yeah, right. Like them."

Few listened, most hurled paper wads trying to force him to abandon his quest.

"My Grandma Nizzie says if you can't make time for God, don't expect Him to make time for you."

"Wow, your Grandma Nizzie's deep. All you Kentuckians like that?"

"Now you're making fun of me."

Scoffers cackled to drown out the lawn preacher. But he persisted nonetheless, for he saw sinners amongst them.

When I failed to force Missy to move her feet, I decided to leave her standing until she got the message. She was getting caught up in the religious mush this guy was spewing.

"So now we have two Hare Krishna preachers on campus. Let's get them together for dueling preachers. Have a big bash at the Union—call it the battle of the Ranhurst Jesus freaks," I muttered while I strolled away oblivious to the preacher's words.

Missy said nothing as she ran the few steps to catch up with me. Her jaw tightened; her eyes shot daggers at me.

"They're not Hare Krishnas. And don't make fun of people who believe in God," Missy snapped.

"Sor-ry, I'm just not into religion. Show me something I can see or touch, then I swallow the story."

"My Grandma Nizzie says…"

"That's okay," I shot in to cut Missy off, "let's save *that* little gem of Nizzie wisdom for another day."

I coaxed Missy back in the direction of Camp Pendleton and out of range of the preacher's voice.

"Well, thank you heaps and noodles," Missy muttered, "Hey, do you think that Quenby guy is cute?"

****

I had no sooner plopped my books down on the desk, relieved that the day was finally over, kicked my shoes under the bed and sprawled out on my mattress when a single forceful knock came at the door. No one I knew knocked that way, so I figured this had to be someone other than a dormmate.

Conrad Merrifield stood there red-faced from the heat, mopping sweat from his neck when I answered.

"I hate the heat," he muttered as he entered with clipboard in hand. His radio hissed and crackled on his belt. His lips remained colorless, smileless and rigid. He said nothing, though I could see his eyes immediately working the room in a sweeping fashion.

I retreated to stand at my desk while Merrifield scribbled on the clipboard.

"Her desk?" he asked, leveling his pen like a pointer.

I nodded.

He opened desk drawers and pushed things around with his pen. Again he scribbled on his pad. His eyes hid whatever churned inside his mind. He avoided eye contact while he worked, and I never took my eyes off of him. He then proceeded to the closet.

"Which girl is Althea in these pictures?"

I selected a head shot of Ali. In another snapshot, Ali lay stretched out on a blanket in a bikini that barely hid her secrets. Merrifield stared at that one for a lingering moment. I could imagine what was going through his mind just then.

Conrad removed the two pictures, catching their corners carefully under the clip. Now why would he need more than just a shot of her face? I didn't want to think about the implications.

"Ali's side is on the left, mine on the right. The top three drawers are hers, the bottom three mine. The shelf on the left is hers..."

"Got it."

Again Merrifield scribbled. He opened the top drawer with Ali's clothes and studied the contents without touching them. Then he proceeded through the others. He said nothing the entire time, and I never could detect any facial changes that might offer up a clue as to what was churning inside his head. But evidently he discovered things noteworthy, since he paused every few seconds to record his observations.

I rose to offer assistance when he seemed to be gazing blankly into one of the drawers. He intently compared the contents of Ali's drawers with one of mine. As he stood there, he tapped his pen on the edge of the drawer in a nervous way.

"Very neat girl," he commented.

The inflection implied I wasn't.

"You disturb any of Althea's things?"

"I went through her desk..."

"But you replaced everything as you found it?"

"Yes," I fired back with a sardonic tone.

Merrifield then sat at Ali's desk to record more of his observations.

I would have maimed to know what he wrote, but I was too far away and thought peering over his shoulder would seem obvious.

"Anything out of place or missing when you arrived?"

"Nothing. Nothing unusual."

"Your suitcases?" he asked, indicating under the bed.

"Gray, red plaid and the blue. Ali's are the matched Touristers."

"You make her bed?"

"No, made when I arrived."

"You sure?"

"Yes."

Merrifield raised a brow and jotted accordingly on his pad. He paused to wipe away the sweat beads accumulating on his doughy cheeks. His smoker's breathing rose over the silence. I had to endure the stench of stale cigarette smoke woven into the very fibers of his uniform. I hoped it would not remain behind when he left. I hate cigarette smoke and normally refuse to tolerate smokers for any length of time. Ali hated smokers with an equal passion.

"Your radio?" He pointed to the cassette player beside my bed.

"Yes."

"Althea have one?"

"She listens to music when she runs."

"You were Althea's roommate last year, correct?"

"Yes, roommates since freshman year."

"And you got along okay?"

"Sure...we're close. Good friends."

The words jabbed at me like a lie. Were we good friends? Or did Ali just tolerate me like so many others? In reality, I had no close friends at Ranhurst, and I was presumptuous counting Ali as a close friend. People get on my nerves, and I can be caustic when I let them know it. A negative character flaw. A flaw that kept most acquaintances at arm's length. They say identifying the problem puts you halfway toward solving it. *Yeah right*. I'm not so sure it's that easy. I probably have a dozen other shortcomings that keep people away. Maybe that's why I have this driving need to find out what happened to Ali. I couldn't abandon my only friend, even if she didn't think of me that way. If the situation were reversed, and Ali were sitting here right now, would she care enough about me to do this? My stomach churned at having to face the answer to that.

"Last year, did Ali have many male friends on campus?" Merrifield probed.

"I'm sorry, what?"

"Did Ali have many male friends on campus last year?"

"A few. Ali dated a lot."

"How 'bout a steady boyfriend?"

"Actually, she had more than one, but not at the same time. Well, maybe three...off and on."

"You remember their names?"

"No, not really."

Merrifield scratched at the hair pricking his neck. He gave the room one more concentrated visual sweep. I watched his eyes, hoping to detect when he saw something relevant. They never changed.

"I've got everything I need," he said.

Merrifield's abruptness caught me unguarded. He spent less than ten minutes in the room, completed a standard Ranhurst form and stood ready to shut the book on Ali's disappearance. I could see it in his attitude and feel it in his tone.

"That's it?" There was no way to mask the cynicism in my voice.

"I've got a pretty clear picture here. If I need anything else, I know where to find you."

I rose, waiting while he finished writing. He said nothing more to me, spoke softly into his radio, then closed the door on his way out. I felt like an enormous weight had just descended onto my shoulders. Nobody around here seemed to care that Ali had disappeared without a trace.

And I had learned nothing. Whatever Merrifield uncovered in this room, he kept to himself. Were there clues here that he uncovered yet I missed? I tasked myself to think through every item in our room. There had to be something here to help me.

Not long after he was gone, I examined the same two drawers that had interested Merrifield. What did he see in there? I detected nothing unusual. Merrifield, however, did.

****

Beth arrived later that evening. The arduous and empty drive from Indiana trapped her into endless hours of anxiety. She said she skipped dinner and couldn't eat anyway. She did however, need aspirin for a headache that started a day earlier when I first told her of Ali absence.

Over the next hour, Beth took in every bit of information I could provide, all the while choking back tears that pried into her eyes. In the end, she realized she knew nothing about what really happened to Ali. Nobody did.

All Beth really had to cling to was that Ali's father had dropped her off at Ranhurst on Friday. Ali unpacked and set up her room, then disappeared.

"Ali's responsible. She'd never do this to her family."

Beyond that, Beth said little, did even less. She looked at me with eyes clouded with terror. There could be nothing more devastating than having to cope with a missing child. No information, no answers. I wished there was something I could say, something I could do that could ease the raging fear that must be burning away her insides, destroying everything that was once a happy life.

Seeing Beth as an unraveling bundle of supercharged emotions, I knew I had to assume the aggressive role. I had to *do* something. Inaction debilitates. Do anything! Even if something seems pointless, do it as a way to keep busy and force worry to arm's length. More importantly, find a ray of hope and cling to it with everything you've got. What else could we do?

For a long, dark moment I drifted. Time is so vitally important right now. Steer to the first positive course and stay there, I told myself. *I* had to do something to help locate Ali.

"Did she talk to anyone on campus?" Beth asked, confused. She fought back her tears, replaced them with a soft mewl.

"I don't know." I had to fight down my own tears welling up in my eyes. "Campus security is handling the necessary paperwork. They've begun their investigation, but Merrifield wasn't hopeful," I offered when I regained control.

"Is that what he said?"

"No, but I could tell. He thinks Ali just took off."

"She wouldn't." Beth stopped. She needed a moment before she could finish. "I know her. I know she wouldn't run away. Why...for what possible reason?"

"I know, Beth. Have you thought of anything else that might help? Anything. The least scrap of information could be important."

Beth sought refuge browsing through Ali's things. She touched the clothes, smoothed her hands over a white v-neck angora sweater that she wrapped in her arms.

"God, I don't even know what she was wearing. Do they have a picture?"

"Merrifield took two from the closet door."

I stood at my desk quietly fumbling through my books and papers, trying to locate where I had written down an Astronomy assignment.

"I'm sorry, you probably have work to do. Maybe I should leave and stay at the Union."

"No, stay. Listen, if you want to sleep here tonight, I can take the upper bunk. Ali always takes the upper bunk. This is my third year with her, and I still sleep down below."

"No. I don't think I can handle staying here tonight. Have you learned anything about who Ali talked to?"

"Not much. There are nine Matthews here. One graduated early, another dropped out after sophomore year. Ali dated a guy named Matt last term. I just can't remember his last name. I'm expecting a call, though."

Beth opened Ali's desk drawer, this time shifting the odds and ends around in search of something. Her sudden intense interest stopped me.

"Something wrong?"

"No, I was just hoping."

"By the way, Merrifield asked if anything was missing, anything she brought that isn't here now."

"I really didn't pay much attention. Ali knew exactly what she wanted to bring. Aside from the refrigerator, television, and radio..."

Beth stopped, staring at the cassette tapes in the drawer.

"Have you seen her Walkman? It's a yellow sports Walkman."

"No."

"She takes it everywhere when she knows she's going to be alone. She would have brought it. She uses it when she runs."

I planted that seed in the back of my head. Ali listened to her Walkman when she ran or... when she planned on spending time alone. That implied what?

Beth searched the remaining desk drawers while I checked the closet shelf.

"It's not here. So Ali had it with her…"

"Maybe she went running," I stopped before my words could conjure images of dread.

The telephone rang. Beth stared at it—hopeful.

I answered. Disappointment slipped into my voice and eyes.

"Jackie, thanks for calling back. Last term Ali dated a guy named Matt. No…Matt. You remember his last name?"

My eyes gleamed. My heart revved up. I tightened my grip on the phone.

"Thanks, Jackie. Matt Evans. No, we haven't heard anything. No, I will, as soon as I hear."

Beth rose in anticipation.

"His name's Matt Evans. He's a senior."

With shaking, sweating hands, I grabbed the Ranhurst directory and flipped as quickly as I could to the **M**s.

"His name's in the directory. He's a Delta Rho."

"You think he called Ali?"

"Could be, but why? He's not on the track team that I can remember. As a matter of fact, Ali said he was a double major—chics and booze."

"Maybe it will help the police."

"Yeah, but first I'm going to Delta Rho to talk with Matt. Let's make sure he's the one who called her…and find out why. Maybe he can help."

4

Windows

The three story, eighty-year-old Victorian house touted two Greek symbols in black on her second-story white clapboards. Windows. The house was a myriad of windows. Bay windows jutted out on the front and sides of the first floor. Octagonal windows passed light into the staircases connecting the floors, while rows of standing panes populated the two upper floors.

I paused at the door to Delta Rho house with a pendulous mind. *Go.* I shifted my backpack on my shoulder. *Stay.* No movement crossed the stained damask curtain over the window. *Turn around and retreat.*

Grabbing the door handle, I silenced my in-decision.

Inside, caustic heavy metal gyrations vibrated the glass. The screeching voices were like fingernails on a chalkboard to the ear. Their words—when you could understand them—incited violence, hatred. Not my choice of music, nor my kind of people. Frat brats. Stuck-up creeps all after one thing.

I faltered and stopped in the foyer. After a minute, two Rhos pounded up a staircase and careened around the corner in the midst of a wrestling bout. They veered left at the last second to avoid a collision with me.

"Hello, bodacious babe alert, all systems stop, up periscope," the pudgier one said, halting dead in his tracks. He released his companion; his eyes bulged as they homed in on my chest.

"Sor-ry," the other, a freckled, acne-infested, frizzy-topped redhead said. When he smiled the tin on his teeth reflected the incoming sunlight.

"I'd like to speak with Matt Evans?"

"You can call me Matt if you want. Who are you?"

"I'm Van Worten. Can I speak to Matt Evans."

"Why? He picks his nose in class. Did you know that? We've got witnesses. Wouldn't you rather talk to me?"

"It's personal. I'm having his baby."

"Ooh, she put you in the dirt, scuzbag," Pudgy said, all the while coveting my breasts with those hungry adolescent eyes.

The two finally got the message and disappeared down the hall. I saw them stop to talk to two other frats at the far end of the long corridor. When they pointed in my direction, I knew what they must have been saying.

Totally useless frat geeks, I thought.

I waited, growing anxious over the delay and irritated by the loud music's constant grating. They could use this stuff to torture people.

Freckles returned with the two from the hall, turning me over to an older frat brother with raven's black hair. His high cheek bones framed dark, probing eyes that immediately snared mine. I couldn't have turned away even if I wanted to. He was spooky in the way he seemed to be looking inside me. Thin, almost colorless lips offered only a hint of a smile.

I was sure this one couldn't be Matt. I had never seen this guy before.

"I'm looking for Matt."

"I'm Kevel, Kevel Moreland. You want Matt Evans?" he said with a voice as smooth as his swarthy, unblemished skin. If it weren't for his vacant, unflinching stare, I could have become entranced by him.

A smileless, sunbleached blond bodyguard-type appeared behind Kevel. His slicked-back hair gave him a sinister appearance. He folded his arms across his chest while his distant eyes sized me up. He stood erect a whole head above Kevel. His lips formed a horizontal line across his face and his rigid manner proved unsettling.

I avoided his icy stare.

"Matt's not here," Kevel said, never acknowledging the one standing behind him.

Kevel's eyes worked lazily over me, settling on areas that interested him. When he spoke he pulled his eyes up to mine with great effort and not the least bit of embarrassment, and the corners of his mouth edged up into an uncertain smile. His was an unctuous presentation that reeked of a perfunctory offering.

"When will he be back? It's important."

In the ensuing silent moment Kevel assessed me, delving deep into my eyes to reveal the depths of my thoughts. I felt unexpectedly exposed, naked in a sense. His eyes remained unflinching.

At that same time, I caught a glimpse of Kevel's mind churning behind his dark, piercing stare. An eerie chill swam through me.

"We don't know. He left suddenly Saturday afternoon. A family emergency. You can reach him at his home."

"Oh."   My response came spontaneous, revealing. Did he see the surprise-turned-suspicion in my eyes?

Matt's gone also. He calls Ali...now he's gone.

"Something I could help you with?" Kevel inquired. His eyes were now steadfast on mine. They never strayed from me.

Was he reading my skittish mind?

Those lips parted enough for perfect teeth to sneak through.

My heart thumped alarm. The hairs on my forearms rose in response. I needed to swallow but stopped myself for fear it would show me vulnerable to those eyes. Why did I feel this way? Something about Kevel set off a danger signal inside my head. Something commanded that I say no more and leave this place.

"No, it's...a...personal. I'll wait 'til he gets back," I stumbled. The urge to leave this house swelled in me as my throat tightened.

Other students moved into the living room a few feet away. My eyes never left Kevel's. His never left mine.

"Sorry. What's your name? I'll tack a note on his door."

"I...Van Worten, Trish. I'm in the Pendleton dorms. Matt knows me."

Kevel walked me the few steps back to the door, then stood stone-still, watching as I descended the frat house steps.

I refused to look back; I knew what I would see if I did.

The stare from his icy cold eyes wormed its way to my most guarded depths. I felt those eyes on the back of my neck.

Reaching the last step, I heard the door close. His very look intimidated me. How could such a seemingly innocuous exchange prove so disturbing?

5

Dashed Hopes

Beth and I stared morosely across the clutter on an impressive mahogany desk. Captain Merrifield strummed plump fingers on the wood as he reviewed the reports spread in a single layer before him. Each report documented official details concerning Ali's disappearance. Each report served as physical evidence of the school's concern for what had happened to Ali.

Beth's ragged eyes moved from the desk to Merrifield's narrowed and unflinching eyes. She tried to discern in a glance what he had learned since beginning his investigation.

The wall clock's rhythmic tick tapped off the seconds while we waited. More time being wasted. The stifling heat had become bottled up in the closed office. I blinked frequently, seeking relief from the cigarette smoke stinging my eyes.

Beth worked her hands one over the other in a tense way.

Out the corner of his eye, Conrad caught the woman's twitch. He raised his eyes from the papers, gazing over narrow bifocals sitting low on his nose. Sweat rolled down his cheeks. Cigarette smoke spiraled from a nearby ashtray and spread like a cloud overhead. Holding his thoughts, he wiped away the tiny beads of sweat accumulating under the eyeglass frames. Then Merrifield filled his lungs with nicotine and returned the stub to its resting place on the ashtray rim. Afterward, he looked into my eyes, seeing things there I'm sure he disliked, and finally settled his gaze upon Beth.

"We deal strictly with facts. And we have very few at this point." Smoke oozed out with each word. "Yes, we did confirm that your daughter picked up her class schedule at Administration Friday afternoon. Our best guess is after eleven but before lunch."

"What about Matt Evans?" I blurted, abandoning my stoic silence to circumvent Merrifield's mechanical attempt at reciting old information. Another day gone. Still we knew nothing.

Merrifield sat there behind his monolithic desk, spewing his vile cigarette smoke into the air. Sympathetic indifference surfaced on his face; his voice was as coarse as sandpaper.

"Ms. Lanaro, it's time we discuss some rather uncomfortable areas. It may be best if Ms. Van Worten waited outside."

"No. It's okay. She knows Ali."

"Suit yourself."

Merrifield paused, rubbing his forehead while he mentally lined up his questions. The time had arrived when he had to say what most parents refused to accept about their children.

"Was Althea a rebellious adolescent? I mean, could Ali have run away to spite you?" he started.

I swallowed my smoldering anger over Merrifield's callous implication. He wanted her to say something that would justify his own conclusions.

"No." Beth responded without hesitation. "She had no reason to run away."

"Were there problems at home? Frequent arguing?"

"No. None."

"Ali would never have bothered to pick up her schedule if she planned on running away," I forced in.

"Was Althea a troubled child? Her record indicates she's a bright student. Was the pressure too much for her to handle?"

"No."

"Could her father have done something to her. You said he drove her to Ranhurst that Friday?"

"No. Certainly not. Are you implying?"

"Taken her with him? Forced her against her will for any reason?"

"This is ludicrous. He'd never do anything like that."

"You're divorced, correct?"

"Three years. He rarely visited Ali after high school."

"Okay. Did Ali have a steady boyfriend over the summer? Did she stay away overnight for any reason?"

"She dated, spent a few weekends with girl-friends but nothing unusual."

"How often was she away for the weekend?"

"Two or three times. She always returned Sunday night for work on Monday."

"What about Matt Evans? Ali dated him last semester," I injected into their exchange. I need-ed to get Merrifield on track. His line of question-ing was going nowhere.

"Matt Evans," Merrifield said, holding on to the name.

"Yeah, Matt Evans. I called you with that the other day."

"I'd like to hear the story from you, Ms. Lanaro." Conrad turned his attention to Beth in a gesture meant to quiet me.

"Someone called Ali, I thought I heard her say the name Matt."

"But you're not certain."

Conrad was more than asking—he clung to the uncertainty.

"No, I'm not certain."

"Then it could have been Mack, or Man, like hey Man, how you doin?"

"I believe she said Matt, for Matt Evans," I in-terrupted.

Merrifield's eyes never left Beth's.

"Had this person called her any other time… that you are aware of?" Conrad directed the flow back to Beth.

The tension across the desk was thicker than the cigarette smoke hovering over our heads. Beth and I felt the heat with every breath we took.

"He could have. I just don't know! Many of her friends called her over the summer."

"Ms. Lanaro, did she ever talk about a boy named Matt either before or after that call?"

"No."

"Think hard. It could be important."

"She didn't talk about him at all. She just told me it was a friend. A few days later, she said she had to report early for track."

"Oh yes, the track coach, Mr. Benjamin Makmohattam. The track team calls him Coach Mack, don't they?"

"Ali calls him Coach Benji," I corrected.

"Now, Ms. Van Worten, you say Althea dated a Matt Evans."

"Yes, in the spring. They went out a few times. Then nothing. I didn't think it was anything serious."

"Why is that?"

"It only lasted a month. And I didn't see them together that often."

"How about other guys? Did she date other guys here at Ranhurst?"

"Quite a few."

"Any serious?"

"None that she confided in me."

Silence wove its way through the layers of expelled cigarette smoke from Conrad's last drag. He scribbled three lines along the bottom of a report. I eased forward hoping to catch a few of the words. They were too small to read upside down.

Beth grabbed the armrests so tightly that her knuckles paled. She had to force the air in and out of her lungs. I didn't know how much more of this she could withstand.

"We're checking every detail you've given us. As I told you when you came in, there is no new information."

"Matt Evans called Ali. He's left school," I said, leaning forward in my chair. I sensed Merrifield's discomfort with having to deal with me. I wanted answers. It seemed he had none to offer.

"We know, Ms. Van Worten. He's at home because of a family emergency. You see, Ms. Van Worten, we're doing our job. We're doing what we're supposed to do. Anyway, what do you know of that?"

Merrifield's eyes locked on mine.

"I went to Delta Rho to speak with him. He wasn't there."

Merrifield tightened his jaw while he took a final drag on his cigarette. His eyes never left the stream of smoke rising. Then he crushed the butt out in the direct center of the ashtray. The action masked a nervous twitch I detected in his hand. The heat, *or something else*, was causing sweat to roll down his cheeks. I hoped my insistence made him uncomfortable. I didn't know what else to do. A friend's life could be at stake.

"Matt Evans left by bus Saturday night. And he didn't call Althea Goodfellow at any time since breaking up with her," Conrad said, his eyes locked on me.

"How do you know?"

"I spoke with the boy on the telephone, that's how I know. That's my job. Is there anything else you need to know, Ms. Van Worten?"

Merrifield drove his point home by dropping a file onto the desk.

I receded into my chair, stifled by the heat and the lingering cigarette smoke. I avoided Merrifield's uneasy glare. Why was it so difficult to accept that Matt was not the one who called Ali? Because he's not here to say it to my face, that's why.

Beth's eyes bounced between us two in that tense moment. She wanted—no needed—to know what had happened to Ali. And neither of us were helping.

"Is there any other information you can offer, Ms. Lanaro? Names of friends back home or places where she might go?"

Merrifield waited.

I wondered for what.

Beth shook her reply. Words were impossible to get out.

"At this point, we're confident Althea has left campus."

He sounded resolute, as if there were no room for doubt in his statement.

"How do you know?" I pressed.

"It's simple, Ms. Van Worten," Conrad started.

My defiant tenacity was about to pay off. I sucked in a breath, focused on Merrifield. My needling had forced him to reveal something only he knew. Inside, I quieted the rush of adrenaline.

"If someone were to become a target of criminal intent, it is highly unlikely they would have taken the time to gather up their toothbrush, toothpaste and makeup. Althea's personal articles were missing from her room. Therefore, Althea must have intended on leaving campus after her arrival. For all we know, she may have departed right after picking up her schedule."

Success! That's what Merrifield saw in those drawers.

"To close the file on this Matt Evans, I interviewed him by telephone. And two fellow frat house students corroborate his story. They drove him to the bus station Saturday night. I have ruled out any connection between Matt Evans and your daughter, Ms. Lanaro."

"Is there *anything* we can do?" Beth asked. A mother's helpless desperation crept into her voice.

"Nothing ma'am. We're doing everything possible to locate your daughter. I've alerted police departments, hospitals, and emergency care centers statewide. If Althea has a run in with the police, or if she's injured or under treatment, we'll be notified."

Merrifield paused.

I sensed Merrifield had held something back, something he was about to produce. Fear choked off my lungs.

"You have to look at this thing in the light of day. We know your daughter was here Friday around noon. We also know she planned to leave campus. If she left alone, she might have gone to visit someone before the start of classes. If she left with someone else, obviously someone she knew, we may never track her down. Throughout our investigation, we have found no one who has seen her after around twelve to twelve-thirty. If Althea decided to take off in search of her dreams, we'll never be able to locate her, and that's not our job. More likely, Ms. Lanaro, she'll contact you. Until then, we'll continue to do everything we can."

Beth mustered the strength to rise from the chair. She shook her head as if to dismiss any theory professing Ali to be a runaway. But what else was there to do? Her daughter had disappeared without a trace, and the police wanted to write it off as a runaway. Case closed. Life goes on like nothing happened.

I wanted to scream.

"Ms. Lanaro, the best thing for you right now is to return home. There is nothing you can do here. And if Althea were to call, she'd call home first."

Beth abandoned her battle to hold back her sobs, turning her face away from the captain.

I said nothing and steadied Beth with my hand.

Merrifield had said all there was to say. Beth and I left him standing helpless behind his desk.

6

Solve For X

I pushed around an untouched and now cold strip steak at Staley's Steak Pit restaurant on the county road not far from the campus. Beth had a driving need to get out of sight of Ranhurst. The baked potato on my plate went uneaten. I despised cafeteria food, and yet I could not force myself to eat what was before me. I also avoided looking directly at Beth, who struggled to maintain a tenuous hold on her courage. She had awakened in the middle of a horrendous nightmare, and now had no inkling of how to escape it.

Neither of us spoke.

I felt helpless. Ali was gone. Nobody knew where. Nobody had the vaguest idea of what really happened. And nobody really cared. Merrifield's responses lacked genuine concern. Certainly Ali left no trail to follow. Or did she? As far as I knew, only one person had seen Ali on campus.

And that left me drifting without direction.

I knew in my heart that Ali would right now be doing everything possible to locate me if the situation were reversed. I had to persevere, even if I was the only one who cared enough to investigate Ali's disappearance. And I felt completely alone at this moment.

"What should I do? If I go home and...I'm afraid to go home," Beth said.

"When will Ali's father arrive?"

"Tomorrow, I hope."

"Wait until he gets here. Go to the dean together. Make them do something."

The force behind my words seemed to foster Beth's strength. Do something—that's the key. We have to *do* something.

I replayed Merrifield's conversation over and over in my head. I refused to believe him. Ali would never take off. Even if she did, she would have confided in someone. Ali had friends. Someone, somewhere, knows exactly what happened to Ali. I resolved I would find that person no matter what I had to do.

"*We* have to find Ali. She's in trouble, I know it. I know she wouldn't leave without talking to me," Beth blurted as if the words had overran her mind.

"Beth..." I started, my eyes gathering tears that must have caused them to sparkle in the candlelight. I reached across the table and covered Beth's hand with mine.

Should I say it? Should I say what was swirling inside my mind? Would it hurt more than help? My bottled anger burned like a torch. I was confused and frightened.

"Beth, there's something wrong here."

Beth became lost in the words. She opened her mouth to speak but stopped, diverting every ounce of strength to fend off her urge to scream.

"We don't know for certain Matt Evans called Ali, but that's all we have to go on right now."

"But Captain Merrifield said he talked to the boy. Matt said he didn't call Ali."

"Okay, suppose he lied. If Matt did call Ali, isn't it strange Matt's gone, too."

"What if I'm mistaken?"

Beth's doubts chipped away at my fragile conviction.

"He's not gone anyway," she continued, "he's at home. The captain said he knew about that."

"I know, but it's still a very big coincidence that Matt gets called home on an emergency."

In the silence, Beth pushed her untouched plate away. We needed answers more than we needed nourishment. Food was secondary, everything was secondary to finding out what happened the day Ali returned to campus.

I refused to accept Ali's disappearance and Matt's departure as disparate coincidence. They must somehow be linked, despite what Merrifield says.

****

A ringing telephone pulled me out of bed. It was 2:30 A.M. and I wanted to sleep. The phone calls were flowing in at three to four an hour, and my nerves were fraying. Now all I wanted was peace and quiet.

In a slumberous stupor, I held the phone to my ear, but said nothing.

"Hello, Patricia...Van Worten?" a gusty southern male voice asked.

"Yes."

"Matt Evans. I understand ya'll been looking for me."

My eyes sprang full open. My mind snapped alert, honing in on the voice.

"Matt. I...ah...I wanted to know if you had called my roommate, Ali Goodfellow?"

"Ali? So you're the one."

"I'm sorry?"

"The one who got the Keystone Cops in an uproar. I talked to Captain Merry-go-round. He asked all kinds of questions about Ali. Hey, we dated for a while, but that was it."

"So, you didn't call her over the summer?"

"I haven't talked to Ali since we broke up. Why?"

"She's missing. And I...we thought maybe you had talked with her."

"Hey, no, sorry to hear she's missing."

"Are you back at school?"

"No, still at home. My old man had a bad wreck. I'm hanging around until he's out of the hospital."

"I'm sorry to hear. I hope your father is better soon."

"Thanks. Hey, sorry if I sounded gruff. I was just pissed that the comedy cops were looking for me."

"Matt, thanks for calling. I needed to hear you weren't the one that called Ali."

"She'll turn up. Ali's always been flighty. A nice chick—a little self-centered—but nice. Good-bye."

"Yeah, good…" I said, hanging up the phone.

****

Beth and I spent three useless hours the following day waiting to speak directly with the Wayne County sheriff. After long delays and excuses, we finally sat before the commander.

He informed us politely and sincerely that unless Ranhurst requested assistance, they would leave the investigation to those best capable of handling it. He further assured Beth of Merrifield's impeccable qualifications and asserted that the captain would investigate her daughter's disappearance thoroughly. These situations take time, he cautioned, and diligence.

His lecture, citing statistics about the thousands of kids reported missing every month, did little to ease Beth's fears.

After remaining stoically silent while I regurgitated all the facts regarding Ali's unexplained absence, he would do no more than advise patience. *Patience and prayers.* The commander was a strict Presbyterian who preached to us that God was just a prayer away. He never put into words that he suspected Ali to be a runaway, but Beth and I read it in his eyes. We exchanged a look of abandonment. Nobody cared enough to take what we said seriously.

Beth had exhausted her patience, and she had long ago turned her back on God.

****

Later that night, I sat on my bed with my books sprawled before me. My mind, however, kept picking apart the substance of the events that had transpired since my arrival at Ranhurst a week before.

Fact: Ali is missing.

Fact: Someone calls Ali a month ago, wants her back early.

Fact: Matt Evans, the possible caller, goes home due to a family emergency.

Fact: He calls me to confirm *he's* not the caller.

Verbalizing that last fact raised a flag of doubt in my mind.

If only I could come up with Ali's activities that Friday. She returned to campus. She unpacked. She took her Walkman and her tooth brush. Why? To meet someone. It *had* to be Matt.

I left my bed and went to the snapshots on the closet door. Was there a face there? Was there something important in one of those pictures?

In frustration, I slammed my fist on the wood. Tears seeped from the corners of my eyes. Tears borne not out of pain but anguish. Something terrible has happened to Ali.

Back at my bed, I took a stab at some Algebra word problems. Concentrating on just polynomials became impossible. Wait a minute. Variables. Solve for x.

X is who Ali saw when she came back. Solve for x. I left my bed to pace. X became a person. I fumbled in my pocket for change for a soda. The stone from Ali's jeans came out with one quarter, a dime and a nickel. Not enough even for a soda. Guilt crept in. Rather than return the necklace, I slipped the stone around my neck. Something inside urged me to put it on. I forgot about everything and admired the stone in the mirror.

I was straying again. But I was still thirsty, so I left the room and sought a drink from the water fountain in the day room. The cool water arced in a clear stream as I bent forward. Then a forked snake tongue shot out and broke the stream. I lurched back with such a sudden jar that I felt my neck crack and a searing pain shoot into my head. I felt my tongue...it was normal and smooth. What was happening to me? I raced back to my room as if I had to hide.

Ensconced in my room, I switched my mind back to Ali. Suppose it was someone other than Matt. Suppose the coach had asked Ali to come back early. Why? A tryst over the weekend? Could Ali be involved with Coach Benji? I contemplated the two making love. Not. Like mixing water and oil.

Thoughts of making love, however, triggered something in me. A tingle rose up from deep between my legs. The same tingle I felt when I made love with Eric back in Chicago. God, it had been two years. Eric, who dumped me right after making love, ruined me in more ways than one for my future husband. Now suspicion and distrust surfaced every time a guy's lips touched mine. He had driven me mad with passion until I caved in. His kisses set me ablaze. His hands triggered an explosion I'll remember forever. Then—slam...bam...thank you, ma'am—he was gone.

Now that same explosion began building anew—exactly how I felt it then. The excitement of his hands against my mound while he kissed my breasts had returned. His...drove me insane with pleasure and left me craving more.

My insides were like shuttle rockets whose engines had just ignited. Ten, nine, eight.

"You're a delicious little bitch."

The words erupted out of my throat and flooded my ears. But that was not my voice.

"What!" I said, losing the excitement that had brought me to the verge of climax.

I doubled over, needing the bunk bed to support my weight. I was panting like an animal in heat. When I shook my head to break what felt like some kind of a trance, long strings of drool whipped from side to side. A knock stole my attention. What was happening? I wiped it away and stared confused at the thick saliva coating the back of my hand.

Before I reached the door, the telephone rang.

"In," I yelled while I snatched up the phone.

Brad was the caller; Colin was at the door.

Last year I couldn't buy a date.

"Sorry, I'm busy Saturday night, Brad," I said, then politely offered a meaningless excuse. It took a stern good-bye to end the call.

"Two-by-four cut down by a buzz saw," Colin said.

Brad (Two-by-four) Callever was tenacious. I would be hearing from him again. This was becoming a test of wills. He wanted me far more than I wanted him.

Colin came alone, saying Quenby had buried himself in his business math books, preparing for a quiz. That reminded me of my Algebra quiz. I needed to stick my head into that book before the quiz. But all I could think about was what Brad had asked over the phone.

"How 'bout taking me to a bacchanal Saturday night," I said after tossing my Algebra book on my desk.

"I love this girl!" Colin said, revealing more than a glint of pent-up desires.

"Delta Rho. Can the Party Meister get us on the list?"

"Get us on the list? Party Meister can do. That's the toughest list on campus, but sweetheart, you can count on me."

My smile raised Colin's alarm flag.

"Hold it a minute," Colin's tone shifted, "*why* do you want to go, anyway?"

"I just need to go."

"You're beginning to worry me. You're not going to get crazy. I got a feeling this is *not* good, but I'll get us into that party."

7

Never Give Up

The next day Beth and I visited the Cleveland office of the Federal Bureau of Investigation. My persistent telephone calls to the bureau proved fruitless. But I refused to fold. The supposed agent I spoke to refused to give a name, saying bureau policy forbade agents from divulging that information over the telephone. So, I would show them. A personal visit might impress upon them our resolve. Somebody somewhere had to care about Ali's disappearance.

The reception we received upon arrival certainly supported my logic. After only a twenty minute wait, a woman led us to an open bay office with a dozen steel desks arranged in two neat rows.

Special Agent Wendell Daniels rose from his desk to greet Beth first, then me. His smile was warm and friendly, not cold and hard as I expected. And when he shook hands his round belly shook ever so slightly. For some reason I had yet to identify, I immediately liked him. By the time we were seated I felt certain this man was going to help us.

He confessed he had been the agent on the phone and complemented me on my professional demeanor despite the gravity of the conversation.

I finally felt a sense of progress.

I harbored a ton of doubt about Merrifield. He intended to do as little as possible to locate Ali. As far as he was concerned, Ali just took off for Hollywood or someplace like it.

The FBI, on the other hand, specialized in finding people. Or so I thought as I stared across the desk at this man. They had a nationwide network of computers and manpower. If any one authority could find Ali, they could.

Wendell's sheepish smile and concerned eyes put both Beth and myself immediately at ease. His voice was quiet and gentle. Hope even began to flicker in our hearts. If the FBI cared, things would happen.

When I finished recounting the facts of Ali's disappearance as I understood them, Wendell held his stone face and politely directed his attention to Beth. I, however, once more detected the sting of sympathetic indifference emerging. It caused my heart to sink.

Agent Daniels had said little.

Beth's story proved too sketchy to add any useful information. All we had to offer the FBI were my suspicions and speculations.

"I sincerely understand how you feel right now. And I don't mean to be insensitive..." Daniels started.

Oh great, here it comes again, I thought, swallowing hard. Even these people didn't care.

"I really wish we could help," Wendell continued as compassionately as possible.

That sincere smile stuck in my throat.

"I really do, but the local authorities have jurisdiction. And from what you've said, it sounds like they're handling it exactly as we would."

"So, you're not going to do anything?" I blurted out, my voice a melange of confusion, frustration and anger.

"Nothing indicates a need for federal involvement in this situation."

Inside, I hoped Wendell was choking on the words. A young woman was missing, while a mother clung to the edge. And from the photograph we produced, he could see Ali was a very beautiful young woman.

Beth began to cry.

"I've been trying to tell you there is something very wrong here. Ali wouldn't have left school on her own. She's not that type. Maybe I'm just not expressing myself well enough!" I shot out with the force of a cannon.

My insistence brought stares from surrounding bureau workers, but I didn't care. We had reached the end of the line. There was no place to go if these people refused to help us. Why can't they understand what we're trying to convey?

"The guy who called Ali has left school! That's not just a coincidence."

"Ms. Van Worten, sometimes things happen just that way—out of coincidence. You, yourself, said he told you he had a family emergency."

"That's correct. But what if he lied? What if he kidnapped Ali?"

"I'm certain the local police will check out every possible bit of information available. They will do everything they can to locate your daughter, that is, if she wants to be found."

A silence hung over the desk while Wendell completed some paperwork.

"I will make certain your daughter's information gets on the NCIC computer network," Wendell offered.

After attaching the proffered snapshot to a Missing Persons report, Wendell escorted us back to the lobby. If we only knew how many of these reports get filed in the state each year... thousands. How many get acted upon? Only God knows the answer to that.

The aura of the FBI that I built up in my mind over the years had evaporated. Beth and I left Cleveland with the same emptiness we had when we arrived. Our persistence gained a sympathetic ear—nothing more. The agent's dismal response extinguished the glimmer of hope we had nurtured during the long drive. Now, even the FBI turned their backs on Ali.

****

Tad arrived with the sun on Friday morning. We joined him outside the dorm and proceeded to the Dean of Students' office where a staff of people had gathered and sat waiting in a conference room. Tad and Beth went inside, Merrifield asked that I remain outside in the waiting area. They would ask me in *when* I was needed.

Their discussions escalated into bursts of anger and frustration at times when Tad accused the school of failing in their responsibility to safeguard the students. Dean Jensen, in a voice of equal amplitude and force, reminded Tad that Ali was an adult and had the freedom to go and do whatever she pleased.

I had been sitting in the chair over an hour, fuming over Merrifield's demand that I not be present in there, when Beth came out the first time. She was ragged and worn. She took the chair next to me, grabbed my hand so tightly that I lost feeling in my fingers, and she looked over at me with eyes that begged for answers.

It seemed after a few moments of my silent support, she gained strength and could return to the conference room. After taking in the bits and pieces I could overhear of Merrifield reciting what he had placed in his reports, Tad bellowed in such anger that the glass door vibrated. No one had answers. And Tad was holding them personally responsible for Ali's safekeeping.

From what I could hear, Merrifield never wavered from this theory that Ali left of her own free will. He probed Tad over and over, hoping to uncover something that might appear as an early warning sign of Ali's intent. Parents are usually the last to realize when trouble is brewing in a teen's life. The Goodfellow case seemed no different.

Dean of Students Jeffrey Lawrence eventually convinced Tad that Ali's disappearance could never have been a prank. If it were a prank, the guilty parties would certainly have ended it long before it reached crisis level.

By afternoon, three hours of me sitting in that blasted chair, Merrifield, Jeffrey Lawrence, and the county sheriff convinced Beth to return home. A week had passed since Ali disappeared. No one on campus could confirm seeing her since that Friday.

Merrifield's men searched the surrounding woods twice, and both times found nothing. No bits of clothing, no discarded personal items. Not a single sign to indicate an abduction.

From where I sat, I could hear most of what was being said, I just had no way of voicing my feelings to those concerned. And it seemed *that* was exactly what Merrifield had hoped to gain by excluding me over Beth's objections.

Devoid of the strength necessary to continue his argument, Tad abandoned his endeavor to convince Merrifield that Ali would never run away. Kids with problems ran away. Ali was a normal, well-adjusted person. At least she never confided in him otherwise. Beth and Ali had a healthy mother-daughter relationship, Beth injected when she could muster the strength to speak out.

By six that night, exhaustion brought silence to the group. So much had been said that it all ran together inside my head. I felt like I was on an unstoppable roller coaster raging wildly out of control.

Merrifield assured Beth and Tad that his office would continue to investigate and would search when the investigation warranted it. However, he remained staunch in saying that if nothing turned up in the next few days, he intended to suspend the operation.

Hearing those words must have sent Beth's heart into a collapse. How can they just forget about her?

I went over what I had heard a dozen times. Yet, I still had no inkling of what really happened. Ali dealt with pressure head on rather than shirk from it. So why run away? What could she be running away from?

Time had erased Ali's tracks.

Before leaving the conference room, I heard Beth urge Tad to bring in a private investigator. Hire some-one experienced in tracking down missing kids. Merrifield was quick to point out that Ali was an adult. She had the maturity, and resources, to go anywhere, or do anything she wished. Gradually Merrifield convinced Beth that outside involvement would only hamper their own investigation.

Tad agreed—but for a different reason. He said a fifteen thousand dollar retainer would be required up front. He had inquired before arriving on campus. Finding runaways was expensive.

8

Party Time

A rainy Saturday dawned over a soggy Ranhurst College.

A sombrous air hung heavy in my room. Before leaving, Tad sat in Ali's chair, cataloging every detail I offered. He knew Beth would miss more than she would remember. Nothing made sense. Especially Merrifield's stubborn insistence that Ali had run away.

I watched the rivulets of rain trickle down my window as the two joined cars eased out of the parking lot. Tad was towing Beth's car, since she seemed too shaken to drive.

Merrifield had successfully maneuvered to keep me in the dark. I knew only what Tad related to me. I kept secret my suspicions that Merrifield had all along manipulated the situation, thereby preventing me from voicing my feelings. I could raise questions no one in that room wanted to answer. I could substantiate Beth's claim that Ali met someone on campus.

At times, I withheld bits of information from Beth and Tad. Most of what raced through my mind was speculation. And Merrifield would find a way to negate anything I said anyway.

Now guilt burned inside me. I doused it with a steady stream of rationalizations. My mind became so muddled in unknowns, I wondered if everything I believed had sprung out of my 'cop show' consciousness.

Seeing them drive away in the out-of-focus blur through the rain on my window, feeling the black void of the empty room caving in around me, and knowing Ali would never act so irrationally, all combined to crush my spirit. I wiped away the tear that found a path down my cheek.

I commanded myself not to cry. Then I cried. Little would get done today.

****

By evening the rains ended and a slate curtain drew back to reveal a sky crowded with stars. Tepid evening air brought relief from past heat. A great time to be outside enjoying the pleasant night.

Colin, Quenby and I arrived at Delta Rho house. We had to slip quietly out of my dorm to get past Missy unnoticed. Colin had refused to go if Missy invited herself along. The frat house interior looked like bodies had been poured in until they spilled out the front door. Even a broom stick would be hard pressed to find standing room inside.

Thundering rock music pumped out the open windows and flooded the neighborhood.

"I hope we're on the list," I whispered as we filled in behind giggling Bleats preening themselves. Freshmen are *so* annoying.

"So do I," Colin jested.

I swallowed an eruption of coppery-tasting fluid. What was I doing? My heart clogged my throat. Why was I here? In that tense moment, I hoped we would be turned away.

"Trust me," Colin replied with a squeeze of my hand.

My face paled in the dim bulb of an overhead porch light attended to by flies and moths. Colin never noticed my nervous smile.

A glint of doubt, however, had surfaced in Colin's words. A doubt his eyes had successfully masked.

"Colin, I may need you tonight. Please don't get sloshed, okay?"

Colin's a good friend sober, but when he drinks he gets out of control and becomes not only useless but at times frightening. I knew that well enough from our previous experiences together.

I slid a warm hand over Colin's. He interlaced his fingers with mine. I felt a sudden warm rush inside. I realized I had never been this close to him before. Maybe there was a chance for him after all...if only he demonstrated more self control.

"I'll be there," he whispered. His lips brushed a delicate kiss across my cheek. He filled his head with my fragrance. I felt suddenly stronger, though I detected a strange look in his eyes. Concern rushed into my head.

Quenby peered with apprehension beneath excitement at the sheer bedlam of flesh within. This party could shoot to number one on his list. Who would have thought American college could be this wild? From what we spied through the windows, Delta Rho would harvest a bumper crop of pledges.

At last we arrived at the door. As expected, a gargantuan half-ape obstructed the entrance. He brandished a clipboard stuffed with ruffled, dog-eared pages as if it were some kind of holy book.

I swallowed hard.

"I hope this works..." Colin whispered, sucking in a breath.

Inside, backing up the gate keeper, two muscle-beach gladiators sucked down beer from long-neck bottles. Their eyes solicited an open dare to crash.

"Trish Van Worten, I'm on your list," I stated simply and directly, then edged forward to wedge inside.

"Babe, you're the *only* one on my list," he replied.

Gargantuan's eyes never went to the clipboard. They grazed over me, drinking in my curves like cheap whiskey and staring at my breasts as if they were abnormal in some way.

"Yoo-hoo, I'm up here," I said.

His smile proved as clumsy as his sidestep to allow my entry.

Colin squirmed in behind me.

A hairy timber arm shot across the opening. Gargantuan wedged granite shoulders between me and Colin. The maneuver trapped Colin and Quenby as anxious girls closed in behind them, blocking retreat.

"We're with her," Colin said, exuding smug confidence.

"Sure Dick Brain. Your name on the list? If your name ain't on the list, I'm gonna be pissed."

"Oh, yeah sure, we're on your list. Colin Black and Quenby Clangston. I know we're on the list."

"When I get pissed, I get mean!"

Gargantuan took a long drink from a half empty bottle of Southern Comfort. Then he shifted his glare to Quenby. "Little weasel," he said.

My eyes sent that *don't-leave-me-stranded* stare.

Colin smiled. Quenby's face became parchment.

"Hey, Dung Bucket, I don't see your names. You're not supposed to be here. You crashing?"

The gladiators shifted their interest to the door, flashing haughty smiles of pure menace.

"No man, we're on the list. Check your pages."

Gargantuan tightened on a fistful of Colin's neon surfing shirt. Colin remained stone-still, his face a snapshot of fear.

"Come on, guys, they're with me. They're my ride. Can't you let them in?" I offered.

"They're not on the list."

Colin delicately covered Gargantuan's hand in a gesture of complaisance.

Gargantuan winked recognition.

In that moment, while Gargantuan's bulk shielded their transaction from the other two, I watched an eight ball of cocaine pass into the fist. Only Quenby and I witnessed the exchange. So, that's how Colin got into these bashes. I wondered at that moment just how deeply Colin had gotten involved into that stuff.

"You're okay. You're on the list. I'm just jerking you guys around," Gargantuan said with an oafish laugh.

After Gargantuan released the shirt, Colin and Quenby slithered through the crack left by the receding giants. With a sigh of relief, they squirmed inside the serried, pulsating frat house. An electrifying energy seized us all the moment we stepped inside.

"Okay, we're in. So now what?" Colin asked.

"I'm not sure," I said.

"We may never leave here alive," Quenby exalted as his eyes traveled from one beauty to the next. They screeched to a halt on three petite Bleats rubbing their way past him, their faces alight with giddy smiles.

Each measured him as they inched along. Quenby must have thought he had just entered that place called Heaven.

The forced sensual contact intoxicated Quenby. The urge to reach out and touch these beauties was almost too much for him to resist.

"Hello ladies, I've just arrived from England. Don't know a thing about your wonderful country. Care to show me around?" he said, painting his face with brilliant splashes of innocence.

"Colin, I'm going to look around. Please don't drink too much. P-l-e-a-s-e," I pleaded.

Colin switched on a smile meant to appease my concern.

I knew it was time to worry.

After being stalled for some time near the front door, I threaded my way into the living room. I had penetrated no further than ten feet in the last twenty minutes. The slow going knotted my stomach. I needed a few deep breaths to quiet the churn inside. What could I hope to gain here?

In the living room, a bearded Delta Rho handed me two bottles of beer and a proposal to find a nice quiet room upstairs. I used one of the bottles to block his kiss.

Strange lips shall never touch mine, I thought. Who knows where those lips have been.

Quenby, likewise, filled each hand with a beer bottle, then swam off like a shark in a sea rich with floundering prey. He abandoned his repertoire of 'pick-up' lines prepared especially for these beauties. Just let the old British accent weave its magic.

Forty minutes later, I stood midway between the front foyer and the rear staircase. Patiently, I picked a path through clogs of drunken students. I had one goal: Reach the stairs leading up. During it all, I clung to my reason for coming in the first place.

Matt's room was up there. And hopefully in there I would find something linking Matt to Ali.

In fraternity hierarchy, juniors and seniors always populated the upper floors, while freshmen and sophomores slept in the basement.

Matt most likely roomed on the second floor. At least that's what I hoped.

I squirmed through a myriad of sweating flesh. The house felt like an oven. Sidestepping drunken passes, not forcing my way, I unobtrusively drifted with the flow.

Finally, I stood at the first stair and looked up. The drone of inane conversations all running together churned inside my head. The cigarette smoke hovering over the crowd was suffocating me. Bodies flowed with the ebb of the party, dancing when a square foot of space became available. Those in stupors gravitated into the corners, where walls would hold them erect. The noise, smoke and commotion all jack-hammered in my head until it throbbed.

When the *'Macarena'* began, the house erupted into sing-along and everyone tried to do the dance despite having no room to stretch out their arms.

I stopped dead in my tracks. Two-by-four!

"Hi Brad," I said, swallowing guilt.

"Trish," Brad responded, not excited, not angry, not anything. At first he smiled, then he tucked it away for another when he realized I had stiffed him. Sure I wanted to go to the frat party—just not with him. Though still early on the party clock, Brad's pupils had already become lost beneath an alcohol and drug-induced glaze.

Midway up the staircase, I turned and scanned over the crowd for Colin. I needed some reassurance before going on. He sat on a table along a far wall in the living room with a bottle in hand. His eyes never strayed from a leggy red-head leaning against the mantle. Then, as if he sensed my stare, Colin looked up to catch my eyes. He never meant that seductive smile for me, only his wink of recognition.

Cackling coeds coagulated in the center of the second-floor hall. Some drifted in and out of rooms, while others flowed down the stairs to rejoin the main party.

The air stunk from pot. When they said an open house, they meant it.

"Matt Evans," I whispered. My whole reason for being here.

A gangly bleached-blonde with angry eyes pushed past me on her way to the stairs.

"Bitch," I muttered.

Blondie flipped me off and continued on.

I eased around a knot of chattering girls encircling two guys. The unmoving flesh choked off the flow in the hall. I paused at a set of doors. My eyes masked apprehension. I detected sounds of passion inside the room on the left. Not that one.

I listened at the opposite door. All quiet inside. I tried the door handle. Unlocked. At the last second, though, I lost my nerve.

A door opened at the end of the hall. I squeezed through to see if that one was Matt's. A threesome blocked my way. And thank God they did. I craned my neck to circumvent the blockage. Kevel Moreland exited the room.

Heart pounding, I eased back behind the three who now shielded me from Kevel. Had he noticed me? Just seeing those dark eyes raised the hair on my neck. Time stopped. I waited. Kevel worked through the crowd, his smile as empty as his eyes.

I turned away as Kevel passed. He never bothered to look. Others peeled back at his approach as if he held power over them. Maybe he did? Every girl there stole a glance as Kevel made his way to the stairs.

I slid to the next set of doors. The door on the left had notes tacked to it. I stared at one. Matt's room!

Now what? My hand stopped a finger's breath from the knob. Everything inside me urged me to turn and leave this place *now*.

I refused to listen. Ali and Matt had to be linked together.

If I stopped right here, I could just walk out. On the other hand, once I entered that room, and if they caught me going through Matt's things, I'd be in way over my head.

My hand trembled. My mouth turned cottony. Any second I thought I would lose my dinner.

A couple exited from the next door over, the girl straightening a rumpled blouse.

"Where's the bathroom?" I asked, spinning around to hide my intent.

"Last door on the left," he said, burying an interested smile.

After locking the bathroom door, I sat on the toilet lid and wiped away the accumulated sweat. The temperature had to be a hundred inside the house. So much so, that I gulped down what remained of my second bottle of beer. Though warm and bitter, it steadied my nerves and sated my dry throat.

How to get into the room? Wait until the party thins out? Then it hit me.

I set the empty bottle on the floor, convinced my reflection that I had to do this, and do it now, then I left the bathroom. Coming out, another replaced me and slammed the door in anger.

I retched a few times for effect.

"Oh God, I'm going to be sick."

"You puke, you clean it up, bitch," an indifferent stringy-haired Bleat said, skirting away from me and hurrying down the hall.

I paused at the right door, clutched the handle as if it were the only thing keeping me up, and pushed. Another mild retch and I was inside.

Others clogging the hall must have breathed relief at my disappearance. No one offered to help. Then again, who would want to?

Once inside the dark room, I leaned against the solid security of the wood and smiled. I was in.

Two beds, two desks, a closet and two dressers. On the far desk, a study lamp's neck had been bent over like an ostrich.

I slid my hand along the panel, found the knob and locked the door. For now I was safe.

Time was precious. I assaulted the nearest desk, switched on the lamp and rummaged through papers and books spread over the entire surface.

"Scott. This guy's name was Scott."

So the other had to be Matt's. I crossed, wasting little time and no steps. Wiping away sweat, I switched on his lamp.

Matt Evans. His name adorned papers scattered about. A schedule, a typed list of books, a collection of names, none of them Ali.

Okay, this is Matt Evans' room. Now what? What was I looking for? My mind raced in a thousand directions. I was risking my neck for something and had no idea what?

Stop. Think. What could I hope to find? Something connecting Matt to Ali. My search moved to the drawers. Standard academic paraphernalia: pens, notebooks, junk. I prayed for a motel match book or receipt; anything that might point me in a promising direction.

Nothing. No such luck—only on TV do people get lucky the first time.

I rifled through the side drawers, my eyes missing more than they caught. Again I came away empty. Panic crept in, pushed logic out. I had no idea what to look for.

I operated with a fervid urgency that only clouded my thinking. The fear of being discovered in Matt's room by someone banging on the door left me unfocused. I stopped, sucking in a long, revitalizing breath.

"Think damnit, what are you looking for?"

No answer surfaced. No brilliant revelation like in the movies.

I glanced at the wall calendar. September fourteenth was circled in black. The day meant nothing to me. It must have meant something to Matt. The twenty-eighth had a red line through it. Not a thin wisp of a line, but rather a firm decisive mark like Matt had pressed hard. The twenty-eighth was important to Matt. For now, those two dates meant nothing to me. Matt had also scribbled 'PARTY' in today's box.

Would Matt have marked off those days if he knew he wasn't going to be here? No. Matt moved into his room and spent enough time here to mark up his calendar and make plans for the first month of school. Everything seemed normal for Matt Evans.

That implied a legitimate emergency could have sent him home in a rush.

I teetered on the edge of giving up. My inner voice urged me to slip unnoticed back into the now ebbing flow of bodies out in the hall. The commotion outside had diminished.

As I reached for the lamp, I caught a nervous giggle outside. Someone worked the door handle. I commended myself for locking it. Then keys.

I froze. I looked down at the desk hoping to spot one small clue by sheer will. I saw an envelope addressed to Matt Evans. Something subliminal triggered, even though I had passed the envelope over earlier. No longer any time to think.

I snatched the envelope into my fist. Beneath it lay a photograph of Matt standing with Kevel and Simon. Kevel was wearing a jersey with a duck jumping out of a hoop on it. Don't ask me why I wasted a precious moment staring at it, but I did. I left the desk lamp on, and dashed for the precarious safety of the closet. I slid behind the slatted door and stood breathless, holding it ajar. I wanted to close it completely but sensed they had entered the room. If the door swayed even slightly, I might be detected.

"You lock the door?" an innocent feminine voice whispered amid an inebriated giggle.

I caught narrow slices of bodies crossing to the bed.

"Use that bed, I'll get the lights."

"You can leave them on," the girl cooed.

Not so innocent, I thought.

Come to *ride the bucking bronco*?

Neither wasted time while shedding clothes. Shoes dropped, then jeans. The lovers jumped onto the bed with a giggle and a crash. Moans of searing passion escaped. In the heat, the lovers coupled atop the bed's blanket as I could glimpse their flesh combined in fluid motion. At that point I turned askance and refused to watch any further.

"Oh, Scottie, can I have some love candy," the girl whispered, her words forced between gasps of volcanic excitement.

The motion stopped so abruptly that I receded further into the closet. Had they seen something? Could they sense my presence?

"Damnit, I told you to never mention that, didn't I?" The words barked with the anger of a vicious animal.

Pure silence.

Then movement resumed. The mattress creaked under the force of their lovemaking.

"I'm sorry, Scottie, I'm sorry. I just wanted a little. I'll give you whatever you want. Please, just give me some. God, I want it so bad."

I listened, terrified now that even my shallow breathing permeated the room. The long moment between the two lovers hung in angered suspension.

The mattress shifted again.

"Oh yeah, that's it baby...give it to me, oh yeah!"

I wanted to close the door during Scott's moans of ecstasy. My hand, however, trembled so violently that I feared the door was visibly swaying. I hesitated, waiting for the mattress to begin its serenade anew to mask any sounds the door might emit.

After another minute, the rhythm of their embrace returned, slowly at first, then with frantic urgency. I listened to escaping impassioned moans, then gasping as they reached the pinnacle of their lovemaking, and finally their unsuccessful efforts to stifle the ecstasy their voices sought to herald.

"Come on already," I whispered so low that only I could hear it.

Timing my action with the height of their copulation, I pulled the door completely closed. So involved were they, that I could have slammed the door against the wall, jumped on the bed with them and yelled fire, and still the two enslaved lovers would never have noticed.

At long last the creaking fell silent. The final moans of waning pleasure escaped.

Sweat rolled down my face. I felt a sneeze sprouting. I squashed it. My legs ached. Oh great! I had to relieve myself again. The beer. Why didn't I just set the bottle down without drinking it? My mind skimmed over something resembling a prayer, hoping neither smoked. A cigarette now would be a bladder-buster.

Torturous minutes passed. The lovers remained silent.

Had they fallen asleep? Would they remain here for the night?

"Want to do it again?" he whispered loud enough for me to hear.

I shook my head.

"You?"

I crossed my legs.

I never knew this could turn into such pain.

"Say no," I mouthed.

"Let's slip back downstairs for something to drink, then come back up and you can do what you did earlier."

I relished the sweet sound of bodies leaving the bed.

"Scottie, I'm sorry about you-know-what."

The girl's apology struck an uneasy chord in my mind. Why? What was love candy, anyway?

I had to endure for only a moment longer. It turned out to be a long moment while the two shared a deep kiss in front of the closet door.

9

Coming Out Of The Closet

Raucous laughter kept all eyes away from Matt's door. I slipped into a stream of drunken Bleats, all stumbling over each other in typical adolescent macho inebriation. Drinking is *so* cool—until you throw up all over yourself.

A hand took my shoulder. I lurched away, commanding myself to move and not come around to see the face attached to the hand.

"That's one cold fish," a voice called.

I wormed my way to the bathroom.

Relief. Thank you.

Afterward, I hurried down the staircase, picking and choosing my way as if crossing a mine field. I wanted one thing: *Get clear of the house.* A snoring, pimpled geek, splay-legged across three stairs, turned over onto my foot. I eased it out, then lowered it to the next stair. Stoned eyes glared up at my intrusion. The guy's perma-grin indicated he must be tripping out on acid. Another looked like he might have overdosed on something. His eyes were completely vacant. I mean, no one's at home.

The music and mirth raged on throughout the house. As I neared the bottom stair, I chanced to raise my head. My eyes locked like a magnet on Kevel's. In the subdued light, his ebony orbs sent out an undeniably sinister glint.

First came recognition, then suspicion. Guilt must have painted my face, for I was certain Kevel could delve into the deepest recesses of my mind. Somehow he knew what I had done.

Kevel offered an edentulous smile. A smile masking his true intent. Casually, he leaned to Simon, who sat beside him. Words were exchanged. But all the while Kevel's eyes remained riveted to mine.

Simon listened, then swept his gaze over the crowd, landing finally on me. In the crammed room, even with blaring music and the drone of frivolous conversations, I knew exactly Kevel's words.

I remembered the envelope stuffed in my pocket. Was it important enough to chance this? I had a moment of uncertainty to decide. Keep it.

Breaking the embrace of eyes, I cast my gaze askance, over the dancers, seeking the front door. My mind backtracked a path through the myriad of bodies, plotting the quickest route of escape.

The distance multiplied tenfold as I calculated my chances of reaching freedom. I needed help. From those dark, determined eyes, I held no doubts as to Kevel or Simon's intent.

Too soon to dump my acquisition, I thought. Try for the door first. At the last minute, if failure caught up with me, I would dump the envelope out of sight and play stupid.

Where was Colin? I needed him—needed him badly.

Kevel and Simon peeled back bodies to open a crease through the granite of bobbing, carousing students. Slowly, fighting the flow, they swam toward me like sharks against the current, homing in on a flapping prey.

A busty brunette threw her arms around Kevel's neck, offering him more than just a kiss. Her tongue sought his throat while her hand slid down his stomach in search of something else.

He unwound her arms as if they were strings and sent her adrift out of his way. His eyes never once left mine.

I spun around the remaining bodies to leave the stairs. A hundred obstacles clustered between me and the safety of the front door. Luckily, an equal number stood between me and Kevel.

Across the expanse of the living room, I espied a laughing Quenby. He was busy fondling the naked shoulder of the blonde Bleat beside him. I vied for his attention with a frantic wave.

Quenby returned a drunken, uncomprehending smile and an exaggerated wave mocking my gesture. He would be no help to me now.

Terror's knot slipped tighter around my heart. I was alone in a jam-packed house. I watched Kevel and Simon pick their way through the students. When they realized my intent, they shifted to take up an intercepting path. Both kept their eyes locked on me.

Then I saw Colin leaning in the far corner of the living room, his eyes as blank as his mind. He must have dropped some acid. He was useless; he'd never even realize I was there. For all I knew, Colin may have passed out and was now propped up to keep from falling on his face.

I spun again, seeking a friendly face, hoping to find someone, anyone who could help me get out of the frat house. Brad's six-foot-three frame was nowhere to be seen.

Kevel slid in on my flank. His persistence had cut the distance between us in half. His hawkish eyes never left his target.

In a glance, I read those cold eyes. I was his prey. His enemy. He must stop me from leaving the frat house. A diabolic glint shone through those eyes.

I felt an icy terror seep all the way into my soul and knew instantly its meaning.

Kevel's jaw tightened when he realized the crowd would keep him from intercepting me before I reached the door. My frantic surge for the safety of the open gateway was evidence enough of guilt. Kevel needed no more convincing—I was a threat. But what I had learned, or what I had found, he had no idea. But he knew something was precipitating my frenzied flight.

Simon, like Kevel, fell victim to the current moving from the foyer into the living room. Six feet could be a great distance when it became impassable.

In desperation, Kevel signaled his gate keepers.

I spun around.

Rhino! Big and fat, face like his namesake. The great beast of adolescent flesh hulked at the entrance to the frat house, beer bottle in one hand, a mostly empty bottle of Southern Comfort in the other.

In a second, Rhino understood Kevel's gesture.

Like his namesake, the corpulent Rhino lowered his head and plowed into the crowd of merrymakers huddled in the foyer.

Girls screamed. Bodies scrambled. Fists flew in the midst of chaos.

Through it all, slowly and unabating, the charging beast plowed an opening in my direction.

The sudden tumult spawned a melee, which shut down my advance toward the door and safety. As much as I feared the wave of violence rolling toward me, I knew there was no turning back.

Bedlam flowed like a plague, first through the foyer then cascading into the living room, permeating the entire lower floor of Delta Rho house. Wild fists rose and fell, seeking perverse pleasure on the nearest flesh. Boozing and brawling—macho male thing to do at parties.

Through it all I skirted the fighting, trying to sidestep the charging Rhino. Amid the confusion, I reached the rush of air bellowing in through the open door. I had made it!

A massive hand clamped onto my shoulder. I whirled, screamed.

A face wedged itself between me and Kevel's out-stretched arm. I twisted to break free. The unknown knight drove his body in closer to break our contact.

The door was a step away.

Whack!

Kevel's fist smashed the intruder's face.

But the force carried both me and my knight out the front door and onto the porch. Without breaking stride, we whirled about and pounded down the stairs. We dashed across the lawn and past a Wayne County cruiser rolling to a stop in front of the frat house. The cavalry had arrived. At least to rescue me.

Helpless, Kevel and Simon held up at the front door.

I looked back long enough to witness a chilling determination in Kevel's eyes. A moment later, Kevel and Simon receded into the pushing and shoving still going on inside. But before turning away, before abandoning his quest, Kevel burned my image into his mind. I was a threat. But a threat to what?

10

New Hope,
Old Fears

My knight and I sprinted a full block from
Delta Rho house before slowing to a stop. The
din of the party-turned-brawl faded into the se-
renity of a warm summer's night. My knight kept
his face concealed with one hand while fumbling
through his pocket with the other.

Inky blood seeped through his fingers when
we fell under a street lamp's discerning wash.
We stood face-to-face, he standing an inch taller
than I. And I'm only five-three. Okay, so he

wasn't a *tall* knight in shining armor. But he did take that punch for me and that qualifies for knighthood.

"I think he broke my friggin' nose," he said, finally wrestling a crumpled handkerchief to staunch the bleeding.

He turned away as if embarrassed.

"Here, wait a minute, let me look at it," I offered calmly. Inside my stomach convulsed at the sight of his blood. My hand to his forearm brought us back face to face.

Alone on the street beneath the light, his soft green eyes seemed unaffected by the pain. For a long moment he stared into mine, and I thought I detected the glimmer of a smile.

"Oh God, I think he broke it," I said after a cursory examination. I avoided touching it. Under the light I couldn't be sure if it had been knocked out of alignment or if a shadow just made it look that way.

"Thanks...for helping me out back there, I'm Trish Van Worten."

"Yeah sure, my friggin' nose is broke. Damnit!"

I studied what I could see of his unremarkable face and straw-colored, spiked hair. Much of his face he kept hidden beneath the handkerchief while his eyes held mine. Had I seen him before? His face seemed familiar. Maybe he was in one of my classes.

"Oh, I'm sorry, Duffy, Duffy Wentworth."

"I really appreciate what you did. Those guys get crazy when they're drunk."

"Yeah, like tell me about it."

"Like?" I whispered. He must be stuck some-where in the eighties. No doubt a California surfer. No, not the surfing type.

"We can go back to my dorm. I could put a cold compress over your nose. That would stop the bleeding. But I don't know if we can do much for the swelling."

"Oh thanks, that's just great," Duffy said, breathing through his mouth.

"Do you want to go to the clinic? Someone there can look at it."

"Oh, you're not pre-med?"

On the walk to my dorm, I felt in my pocket for the envelope. It was there, safe. If Duffy knew he had taken that punch, with its bloody after-math, for a worthless envelope, he would probably punch me himself.

Yet Kevel seemed—no was—desperate to get his hands on me. Was there something in that old Victorian house? Something having to do with Ali. Something he feared I might have un-covered. That house had to have something to do with Ali's disappearance. I could feel it and con-vinced myself that I wouldn't be frightened off by thugs.

Could Ali actually be in the frat house?

That was crazy. Unless...she was there by choice. Did she see Matt at Delta Rho before she disappeared?

By the time we reached Camp Pendleton, I concluded Delta Rho definitely played into Ali's disappearance. How, and to what extent, I had yet to reason through. Kevel's eyes intimated in-volvement. But how could I convince Merrifield of that? Kevel could be a part of it, maybe at the heart of it. Something deep inside kept telling me that. However, like so much else, these were suspicions—without substantiation. Merrifield already viewed me as irrational and emotional. And maybe I was.

Duffy removed the blood-soaked handkerchief once we were ensconced in my room. The bleeding by now had slowed to a trickle. A few of the girls in the day room took notice of our entrance but had the courtesy not to inquire. You could bet they'd be knocking at my door the moment Duffy left.

A cold washcloth blanketed the swelling on the bridge of Duffy's nose while he stretched out on my bed. I dabbed away the remaining crusted blood.

"I think it's stopped," Duffy said, anxious to get up.

"Let's give it a few more minutes."

He smiled with his eyes, looking like a compassionate bandit.

I smiled back, mine a melange of guilt, and I wasn't sure what else.

"What time is it?" he asked.

"One-thirty."

"What time is guys out?"

"Duffy, lay back and relax, okay. We have until two-thirty. If you're not going to go to the clinic, I think you should stay right there on the bed until the bleeding stops completely. It's the least I can do."

Duffy settled back and allowed his eyes to close.

"Does it still hurt?"

"A friggin' broken nose hurts, okay."

"I'm sorry."

"It's okay," he apologized.

I put my back to Duffy, and concealing my movement, eased the envelope out. A Virginia return address, from a Maggie Sewert. The envelope remained sealed. Opening it made me guilty of tampering with the mail. I could just see my FBI application being turned down for that.

From the creak of the bed, Duffy must have turned to watch me.

Still behind my shield, I tucked the envelope away. What would he think if he found out what I had done?

"I appreciate what you did back there. I mean it."

I combed my fingers through my hair, suddenly self-conscious.

"Trish, can I ask you something?"

A pregnant pause lingered between us.

I raced through possible questions, scurried to line up probable responses. What if he...

"Sure."

"Why was he reaching for you? You his girl-friend?"

I breathed relief.

"No. I don't know, Duffy. I was just trying to get out of there when that whole brawl started."

Duffy rose to a sitting position.

"The bleeding's stopped. I can go now."

"You don't have to. I mean, you can stay a while longer. It's not two-thirty yet," I heard my-self blurting out.

Duffy hesitated.

"No, I better go. My dorm's across campus."

Releasing a moan from the residual pain, Duffy situated himself back on his feet and checked himself in the mirror. Not a pretty sight. He then returned the bloodied cloth to me.

Without a word, he started for the door, but he stopped before reaching for the knob.

"Trish, would you consider going out with me?"

Duffy's request was rushed, clumsy.

"You mean on a date?"

"Yeah. We could go out for dinner or something."

"Sure Duffy. When?"

"Would tomorrow night, I mean tonight, be too soon?"

"You sure you'll be up to it with your nose like that?"

I messed up. After I asked the question, I realized it sounded like I was probing for an out.

"We could go to a movie...nobody will see you're out with a bloated-nose geek."

"Sure Duffy, I'd love to."

"Can I call on you around five?"

I glanced at my books on the desk. I was falling desperately behind. My plan had been to play catchup on Sunday. Now Duffy had changed that.

"Duffy, I, ah..."

"If you don't want to, I understand."

"No, no, five will be fine."

****

I awoke tired after a fitful night. The party had left Kevel's face painted on my mind. But today I would work. No volleyball, no Charlie's, just Sociology, Astronomy and Algebra.

Within an hour, my speculating subconscious forced me to raise up from my books and wander over to the desk.

My drawer held the envelope to Matt Evans. I stared at it, trying to decipher exactly what it was that kept tugging at my concentration like a spoiled little child.

An ordinary envelope, it had an unadorned script. The writing was legible and slanted to the right. I studied the return address again. Maggie Sewert had sent the letter. I already knew Matt came from Virginia. Matt's divorced mother? Matt's married sister? Matt's girlfriend?

The urge to open it gnawed at my mind. If I opened it, I might learn something related to Ali's disappearance.

I held the envelope up, checked the seal. Intact. Opening it violated federal law. That meant even if I learned something, I had to keep it from the police. Or did I? What was more important? opening someone else's mail or my roommate's safety?

I returned the envelope to my desk, pasted my concentration onto Astronomy. I had an evening lab at the observatory on Thursday, then a test the following Tuesday. If I didn't get aggressive, I'd surely fail. If I didn't get aggressive in my search for Ali, then what? Was Merrifield doing anything to find her? Was it all hopeless?

The letter wormed its way to the forefront of my mind again, determined to remain there.

Hi Matt, how's school? And how is that girl you said you were meeting when you got back? Is she cute? What's her major? Is it serious between you two?

I wondered.

That could be the letter's contents. It could connect Matt to Ali. Or it might say absolutely nothing about Matt's relationship to Ali.

Uncertainty stomped all over my mind. Four o'clock was minutes away. I banished my suspicions knowing full well they would refuse to remain gone for long.

****

Duffy was punctual, smiling, and black and blue. A handful of daisies partially obscured the previous night's encounter. Relief overran his face when I answered his knock. I interpreted it as one part happy to see me, and one part happy to see I abstained from hiding under my bed to avoid him.

Discoloration ridged the underside of Duffy's right eye and along his nose. But the swelling already showed signs of abating.

"Does it still hurt?" I said, wincing in sympathy.

"Only when I breath."

Seeing his injury, now so pronounced, rekindled my guilt. Was that why I accepted a date with him? Was this date repayment for his chivalry? And if so, after tonight, was the debt paid in full?

I decided to reserve my answer.

"Would you mind if we ate light, took in a movie, anything but a comedy, then came back early? I have a test tomorrow," Duffy said.

"That would be fine. I'm really behind on my studying. If I don't buckle down, I'm not going to make it past my first Astronomy exam."

Duffy's eyes alighted. Duffy knew a little about Astronomy. Thank God. Someone who could help. Throughout our walk to Charlie's, during dinner and afterward, Duffy tutored me on the essentials of the Cosmos. I marveled at his infectious enthusiasm. And I liked the way his lively eyes concentrated on me when I talked. He really was interested in me. He exuded a charm that wormed its way inside you and before you knew it, you were hooked. And not in that typical macho sexual way. He never once interrupted to try to outdo me. There was no *I'm-smarter-than-you* contest so typical of every other guy I meet at Ranhurst.

At times throughout our evening, I thought Duffy had something he wished to ask, but refrained. Sometimes he made me laugh. Other times he listened to what I said—really listened and really cared. He refused to talk about himself, instead he probed for bits and pieces of my life. I found myself growing excited just from our conversation. I didn't want the date to end.

After leaving the movie theater, as we strolled through the campus, I thought he might finally broach whatever subject had been lurking in the shadows of our date.

The night sky glistened. And Duffy had run out of constellations. The silence between us made his unasked question obvious.

"Can I ask you something...personal? You don't have to answer if you don't want to," he finally presented, at a time when it seemed nothing else could subvert the moment.

"Sure."

"Why was that guy at the frat house trying to get at you? From the look in his eyes, he really had it in for you."

"I don't know..." I started, then sorting through the rush of feelings clamoring helter-skelter inside my head, I chanced to offer the truth.

In the past hours I had come to respect Duffy. Enough to be completely honest with him. Conversation came easy. He spouted no sexual innuendoes, no need to exert his manhood, or to tout superiority over me. He gave me no cause to have to sidestep the male pleasure-dominated psyche. He really was a knight, different from the other guys at Ranhurst.

"I went to Delta Rho house looking for something," I stammered, uncertain of how best to structure my explanation.

I stopped. We were near my dorm. I wanted to maintain our privacy, so I offered an alternate path to lengthen our walk, and our date. I could see this pleased Duffy.

I then restarted at the beginning, telling him of Ali's disappearance and the events surrounding it. I ended claiming the campus police were doing nothing to find Ali.

Duffy listened. When I finished, he said nothing. Everyone else claimed I was paranoid. Duffy didn't. But neither did he jump heartily into my story.

"You learn anything from the letter?" he asked.

We approached my dorm once more.

The question surprised me. I read his eyes—he was serious.

"I never opened it."

"Would you mind if I have a look at the envelope. I mean I did get this over it." Duffy touched his nose.

I smiled, relieved he believed me. I quickened our pace.

At the dorm, I dismissed the stares from the other girls. After all, how does one explain a date with a guy whose nose is black and blue?

"So this is what it was all about," Duffy said taking the envelope while unconsciously rubbing his nose.

"Does it still hurt?"

"Sometimes. Did he know you took this?"

"No. I don't know."

"By the way, the nose isn't broken, but it will be a few days before it gets back to normal."

I accepted Duffy's present condition as temporary. After all, he had taken a punch for me. Beneath those bruises, I suspected I would find a cute face. Now I would have to give it a few days to find out. I realized, however, that Duffy offered much more than just a cute face and tight beef cakes.

"Trish, you said Matt went home suddenly last weekend?"

"Yeah, the guys at Delta Rho said it was a family emergency or something. When Matt called me, he said he was at home. He had left on Saturday. Why?"

"I don't know."

"Ali had said Matt was from Virginia. He had that smooth southern accent and was real polite."

Duffy stared at the envelope.

"Why?" I asked after a long silence.

My single word shattered Duffy's concentration.

"Well, suppose this letter is from his mother, or a girlfriend, or somebody he knew back home."

"Okay."

"Why would it be postmarked on Tuesday. He would already have been home for three days?"

"Let me see that."

I stood beside him to share the letter. I felt his warmth against me. His skin brushed against mine when he tilted the envelope my way. The hairs on my forearm contacting his became charged.

He was looking at me, though I kept my eyes on the envelope. Was I ready to kiss this guy? Everything inside was screaming yes. However, I refused to make eye contact, uncertain of whether he was waiting for a signal from me. And maybe it was too soon.

The postmark town matched the return address.

"How did Merrifield deal with the information you gave him about Matt's telephone call to Ali?"

"He said he personally talked to Matt, and Matt assured him that he never called her. Matt even called me."

"Matt called you?"

"Yeah, why?"

"Where did he call you from?"

"Home, I guess..."

Just saying it raised a flag of doubt in my mind.

"So, what are you going to do?" Duffy asked.

"Find out for myself."

Duffy smiled. Our faces were inches apart. He wanted to kiss me, his eyes betrayed that much.

My eyes flashed approval.

But Duffy floundered, and the moment passed unfulfilled.

With the magic of the moment gone, I grabbed the telephone. After a fruitful minute with a directory assistance operator, I dialed the number. Without thinking about what I would say, I counted the rings. Five rings later, I was ready to abandon the call. But I let the rings continue. On the ninth ring, someone answered.

"Yeah," the callous male voice grunted, angry at the disturbance.

"Hello, can I please speak with," I said, pausing while I rechecked the name on the envelope, "Maggie Sewert."

"Maggie's not here. She's working, won't be back until late. Call back tomorrow during the day, will ya."

"Wait, please. Do you know Matthew Evans?"

My plea snared his attention; he softened his granite facade.

"Matt? Sure, Matt is Maggie's boyfriend, well, fiance. Why?"

"Can you tell me if Matt came by to see Maggie within the last few days?"

"Matt's away at college. Ranhurst in Ohio. If you want to talk with him, contact his parents, they'll give you his number at school."

"Do you know if Matt is at home?"

"Look lady, I told you Matt hasn't been here. Why don't you call tomorrow. You can talk to Maggie then."

"Thank you very much. I'm sorry to bother you."

I hung up with trembling hands. Fear had shackled me.

"What did she say?"

"It was a he, Maggie's father. He said Maggie and Matt are engaged."

"So what else did he say?"

"He said Matt hasn't been there. Matt's at school. Ranhurst College in Ohio."

Duffy sat down on the bed.

"That's why the letter postmarked four days *after* they said Matt went home."

I stared vacantly at Duffy. He saw my mind churning.

"Matt never went home. There was no emergency. Everyone here thinks Matt went home while his family thinks he's here," I said softly, realizing I was right. Ali and Matt are somehow linked.

11

Life's Little Surprises

The Pendleton Courts Student Activities Committee planned an ice cream mixer for Tuesday night. Talk about generation gaps. Students were busy stashing booze and drugs while the faculty thought giving them ice cream would be a wonderful treat. I don't think I'd been to an ice cream social since middle school. Everyone in Pendleton Courts was encouraged to get out and mingle. I remained locked in my room. I really wasn't much for mixing in social situations. Having to smile and be polite while people droned on and on about how wonderful they are and how fantastic their lives are is more than I can handle right now.

I intended to remain sequestered with my books in my room. I turned down Colin's invitation, and by seven-thirty the dorm had become a desolate place. The perfect environment for concentration.

So why couldn't I study? The unusual silence ate away at my concentration.

Before I could force myself back into my Russian book, a rap came softly at the door. Duffy stood sheepishly in the fading light, his smile an oasis in the arid sands of dreaded academia.

"How about some ice cream? I understand there's a mixer going on down the way."

Duffy's smile had lost some of its glimmer against the discoloration beneath his eye.

"I'd love some," I said, surprised he turned up at my door.

My studying had bogged down somewhere between simple Russian verbs and conjugation anyway. Each time I hit a wall, my mind pulled me in a different and unrelated direction, toward Ali's disappearance. So, maybe a break and some social camaraderie would clear my head.

Strolling between the buildings, Duffy's jokes made me laugh. I think he loved the way I laughed—so free and easy—because he worked hard at it.

I looked at Duffy trying to mask my growing desire. I felt so good when I was with him. I almost wished we never made it to the mixer.

"Did you learn anything from the name on the envelope?"

"Get this. Matt and Maggie are engaged to be married when he graduates. Matt isn't at home. Maggie called."

"Then he may have something to do with your roommate."

He may? For sure they were related.

At the mixer, music pulsated from huge speakers set on picnic tables. Students mingled, some collecting into small knots, others roaming about in search of friends. Everyone, though, indulged in the ice cream. The gesture, though small against the evening heat, proved a tremendous lift to student morale.

Duffy and I were standing in the serving line when all heads turned into the fading ochre sun. The girls in front of us all stared in the same direction.

"There she is," one of the girls said.

A volley of ridicule and laughter erupted.

"Who?" her friend asked.

"Catwoman. Our very own Dysfunctional Girl. She's a disgusting retard who rides around campus all the time."

"I'm searching for my cat...." the guy standing with them said in a scratchy voice that mocked Catwoman.

I craned for a glimpse of the unimposing thirtyish woman peddling along the road. Her sweat-stained cowboy hat hid bespectacled eyes. Catwoman. No one even bothered to learn her real name. She always wore faded, skintight jeans, a gaudy chrome buckle, and frayed western shirts.

"Texas is that-a-way, you retard!" someone shouted, hoping to snag Catwoman's attention.

"Fuckin' yuppies," Catwoman muttered just loud enough to be heard.

She habitually peddled the Ranhurst walkways, supposedly in search of her lost cat. Like it or not, Catwoman was as much a part of Ranhurst as Charlie's Café and Peter the lawn preacher.

When Duffy and I turned from the serving table, we came face to face with Colin and his faithful companion Quenby. Instant enmity flashed between Colin and Duffy. The awkward moment lingered.

Neither spoke.

I could see the mechanizations in Duffy's mind working. Duffy had to decide. Back away or stand tough? Staring through granite eyes at Colin, he decided to stand tough. At worst...another black eye. Colin had half a head on him, seemed immovable, and definitely angry. There was, however, no doubt that in Duffy's mind I was worth a hundred broken noses.

"I didn't think you were into geeks," Colin finally said. He never blinked. I hated when he got this way. At least he wasn't drinking this time.

Duffy remained rooted beside me, every muscle in his body tensed in anticipation of another bloody confrontation.

"I guess I was wrong," Colin muttered. His face turned ruddy and he stomped off.

"Colin this is..."

I never got to finish.

"Hi, Quenby Clangston, I didn't get your name," Quenby injected quickly. His hand eagerly grasped Duffy's.

Quenby watched tension drain from Duffy's eyes.

"Duffy...Wentworth."

"I reckon something got his knickers in a twist, wouldn't you say?" Quenby offered, hoping to dissipate the lingering uncertainty.

I said nothing. I was glad to be with Duffy. My smile and a gentle squeeze from my hand let him know it. It was at that moment that I realized I was beginning to fall for Duffy.

But Colin rarely abandoned a quest so easily. From across the way, he watched us regularly, as if tracking our movements, glaring first at Duffy then at me.

Duffy I'm sure sensed they would never become friends. Colin's intimidation kept Duffy uneasy. I assumed that was its intended purpose. But Duffy soon realized Colin's actions stemmed more from a desire for me than animosity toward him.

Competitors both after the same prize. A little competition never hurt anyone, I say.

Colin, however, was not above sabotaging a relationship. Especially where I was involved. I suspect he would continue to solicit dates when he thought he might drive a wedge into our budding relationship or worse. A moment later, when Duffy made me laugh, I told myself I would never let that happen. When I looked around Colin was gone.

The two hours passed like two minutes. Against a fading cinnabar glow, Duffy and I strolled back to the dorm. His hand was warm in mine, and I relished this moment we had together. I thought seriously about pulling out a blanket and laying on the grass together to watch the emerging stars. This night was turning out to be a dream. But we each had to renew our quest for knowledge.

My hand belonged in his. Being with him felt so right—so good.

A discordant throb of rock music emanated from inside the Pendleton Courts dorms. While outside, mosquitoes swarmed around the buildings as if the music were driving them into a feeding frenzy. As it turned out, I was relieved to be inside the building. The blanket idea would have turned into a disaster.

We lingered outside my door, Duffy reluctant to say goodnight. We both knew it was time to get back to work. Both had classes to worry about.

I read his eyes. He really wanted to stay.

"Something to drink? There's a soda in the fridge."

"Okay."

I unlocked and threw open the door.

I froze.

The contents of my room looked like the victims of a tornadic wind. Someone had thrown my room—my entire life—into upheaval. Clothes were ripped from the closet and lay scattered on the floor. What had been in the desk drawers was now dumped into a heap. Even the blankets had been stripped from the beds.

I staggered. Someone had violated my most private place. Someone had trashed my home.

Duffy shuffled his way into the center of the mess.

"Jesus," he muttered.

Tears gathered in my eyes. I began to quake.

"Trish..."

"What!" I screamed, releasing my pent-up tears.

"Take it easy, don't lose it." Duffy took my arms to steady me. "Everything's all right. Somebody just vandalized your room. Probably looking for money. It's okay."

My sobs grew louder. I trembled in Duffy's arms.

"I'll call the police."

By now, a crowd had gathered to peek into my room.

"It's okay, just somebody looking for money," Duffy offered to onlookers. After getting me into a chair, he dialed the number for the campus police.

While we waited, Duffy helped me organize my thoughts. Did I keep money in the room? Yeah right. Was anything missing?

A minute later, Duffy checked the door. When I questioned his action, he dismissed it.

Quenby wormed his way through the girls in the hall to get to my door.

"Hi Trish. I'm sorry, I can see you're in the middle of something rather sticky," he said.

"Yeah, somebody trashed my room."

"I'd say. Quite the malicious chap, too," Quenby replied, surveying my belongings. Seeing Duffy there, Quenby felt out of place. So politely, if not a bit mysteriously, he excused himself and disappeared.

"Have you seen Colin?" I managed to call out as he left. But I was too late.

The security officer, who arrived twenty minutes later, said little while filling out the standard vandalism report. He asked his questions with an indifference that came from completing such forms on the average of a dozen times a week. He saw no significance between this and my concern over my missing roommate.

All these people are incompetent, I thought.

He asked what was stolen.

No money. I always carried what little money I had on me, in my back pocket, so the thief got no cash. Though my survey was cursory, I didn't believe the intruder took anything of value.

However, I had no inventory of Ali's personal property. The big ticket items: television, refrigerator and my radio were still there and the officer duly noted that on the report.

Before leaving, the security officer reviewed each line of the report with me. Everything had been properly recorded. It seemed that was all anyone cared about around here anyway.

Duffy caught up with the security officer in the hall, but not out of my range.

"Will her lock be changed?"

"Sure. I checked the appropriate box on the report," the officer said.

This bold invasion into my sanctuary sent shivers through me. Now I feared being alone in the room. My eyes searched Duffy's; he knew what they meant. Yet there was nothing I could do.

"You want to stay at the Union tonight?" Duffy asked.

I looked at him with vacant eyes.

"I mean by yourself. Get a room there for the night."

"No, it's okay. I'll stay here. I have to put everything back in order."

I began mechanically picking through my clothes, folding each item before placing it back in my drawer.

"Ya'll want me to stay with you...if you're scared," Missy offered.

I accepted. Another body in the room would ease my fear. The last thing I wanted tonight was to be alone.

Duffy, in the mean time, snooped around the closet.

"Is there anything here somebody would want? I mean something that could somehow be involved with Ali?"

"I don't know. There really wasn't anything unusual that I can think of."

Vocalizing my thoughts, hearing the words enter my ears triggered something in my mind. I went to the closet and swiped my hand back and forth at the rear of the shelf on Ali's side of the closet. I came away empty.

"It's gone."

"What's gone?"

"Ali's jewelry box. It's not a box really, it's more like a small oval case, a silver metal case with etched horses on the top."

"Was there anything valuable in it?"

"I don't know. I remember it from last year. Ali kept earrings, necklaces and bracelets in it. It was fairly small, and I doubt if the jewelry had any real value."

Duffy searched through the drawers, then pried around the desk. The jewelry case was missing.

"Could Ali have taken it with her?"

"No. I saw it when I was unpacking."

"You're sure?"

"Positive. It was on the shelf."

I whirled around and went to my desk, searching frantically in silence.

"Duffy, the letter's gone, too."

"The letter?"

"You know, the envelope addressed to Matt Evans."

"Where was it?"

"Here on the desk under my books."

I searched through every piece of paper, every book, and every drawer in my desk.

"It's not here."

We both suspected what that meant. Delta Rho.

****

Two days later, I trudged up the stairs to the office of Student Financial Affairs after an excruciating day of classes. Money problems were the last thing I wanted to have to deal with right now.

The notice in my mail box informed me of an urgent five-thirty appointment with a Mr. Daniel Garrett, who handles tuition records for the college. I can't believe how much they screw up around here. Now they're going to tell me my tuition is delinquent.

Great, that's all I needed today. The notice failed to mention *why* Mr. Garrett wanted to see me, but I knew from experience these things were never good.

"I don't understand why I got this notice," I complained to an inattentive student clerk shuffling through a filing cabinet. She stared at me with vacant eyes for a long moment before speaking.

"I'm sorry, what?"

"I don't understand this notice. I know my tuition and fees are current. My parents sent the money in July."

The clerk stared at the note for a second and shrugged.

Thanks for all your help.

"Garrett's office is on the second floor, last door on the right. Room 208."

I shifted my backpack and left.

The deserted building made my stomach churn. Walking up the stairs alone stirred an uneasiness inside. The only sounds came from my feet. An eerie feeling swelled inside.

I hesitated at the second floor.

Twenty paces ahead the door to Room 208 was open. The sign on an inner office door read DANIEL GARRETT.

"Hel-lo?"

I waited beside a vacant secretary's desk.

"This is just great..."

I checked my watch. Five minutes and I'm outta here. How can this guy make an appointment, then not show up?

"Miss Van Worten?" a burly voice asked behind me.

I jumped.

A brawny linebacker type filled the doorway, folders in hand. He looked at me as if I had done something wrong. I began to feel intimidated despite being unaware of why I was even asked to be here.

"Mr. Garrett? I have this notice..."

"I know. Let's talk in there."

He closed the inner office door and motioned me to the chair while he took up residence behind the desk. What seemed strange was that the desk was clean except for the folders he brought with him. I fought down an urge to get up and go for the door. He must have sensed my apprehension because I stared back at the closed door.

Yet the way he carried himself sparked my curiosity. This one looked nothing like an accountant. I felt suddenly skittish.

"I know my tuition is current. I don't understand why...I also got a letter confirming my grant for this year. I can show it to you..."

"Miss Van Worten, I'm not interested in your tuition."

"Then why am I here?"

"My name is Nick Logan. I'm with the government. I need to talk to you about Althea Goodfellow's disappearance."

"The federal government?"

"Yes."

"So, the FBI is finally waking up. I told you guys this wasn't a runaway case. And I just found out Matt Evans never went home." My initial awe of this man quickly turned to anger.

"Matt Evans?"

Nick released too much surprise in his voice. His face was anything but warm and friendly.

"Yeah, Matt Evans. You guys can't seem to get your act together. I told your man in Cleveland about him."

I repeated the whole story. This time I included my most recently unearthed facts.

Nick scribbled to keep up.

"Wait a minute. Why are you writing this down?"

"I just want to make sure I've got everything straight."

"Matt's a Delta Rho."

Instead of listening, Nick skimmed the FBI report on Althea Goodfellow. Nowhere did it mention a Matt Evans.

"Miss Van Worten, you just stated Ali's mother couldn't confirm Matt Evans was the caller."

"I'm sure he was. No matter what he says."

"What who says?"

"Matt called me a few days after I reported Ali missing. He said he never called Ali. I don't believe him. Evidently Merrifield does."

"Merrifield?"

The barrage of information was proving more than Nick could assimilate. He scratched at his salt-and-pepper hair that was in desperate need of a trimming. He wore an ill-fitting suit, shoes that were scuffed, and a tie dotted with multiple food stains. I always thought FBI agents had to be perfect.

"Yeah, Merrifield said Matt assured him he had never called Ali and hadn't seen her when he arrived back on campus."

"Miss Van Worten, we really want to find Ali. We're doing everything we can. But if I'm to help, I need you to be completely honest. Even if it means betraying a friendship."

Nick delivered a stern all-business glare. He had no intention of taking any bull off of me.

"What are you saying?"

"I'm saying I need honest answers, no matter what."

"Fine."

Nick plowed ahead.

"Did Ali do drugs, either habitual or recreational?"

"No. She's on the track team. Drugs show up in testing."

"Could Ali have been selling drugs?"

"No. And I can't believe…"

"I'm searching for criminal intent here. Bear with me. Was she in trouble?"

"No. Not that I'm aware of."

"What about Matt Evans? He do drugs?"

"You mean did I ever see him taking drugs?"

"Yes."

"No. But drugs are easier to get than beer on this campus. You want my opinion, Matt probably did drugs regularly."

This was getting Nick nowhere. An edge of frustration seeped out. What was he looking for? A link from the missing girl directly into the campus drug traffic. Was he more interested in busting the druggies on campus than finding Ali? Was this creep trying to use me to get at the dealers?

"Were Matt and Ali intimate?"

"I don't know."

"You said they had dated only a month or so."

"Yes."

"And Ali never told you if she was intimate with him."

Nick raised a suspicious brow.

"Correct."

"Was Ali intimate with other men on campus. That you are aware of?"

"No."

Nick cataloged my sudden shift. Maybe Ali and I shared secrets about each other's relationships? Secrets I found too difficult to betray to him.

"Can you provide me the names of guys Ali dated last year?"

"I only remember two other guys. They were both earlier in the year. But yeah, I'll get them for you."

"What about a cult? Could Ali have been involved with any cults on campus?"

"Cult? What are you driving at? Ali is your typical straight-laced college junior. You guys are digging clear on the other side of the hill."

Nick thanked me abruptly, began collecting his papers.

"That's it?"

"Miss Van Worten, we are doing everything we can to find your missing friend. She is not the first to disappear under mysterious circumstances. It is imperative *no one* know we had this little talk. Our investigation could be compromised. Do you understand?"

"Then it's don't call me, I'll call you."

Nick winked.

"I've got your number. I'll be in touch. When I call please have the information ready. For now, I have everything I need."

"Well that really helped," I muttered as I left the building. With government agents like Logan, it's a wonder the FBI is capable of finding anyone.

****

The following day, after enduring the sting of a totally depressing hour in Algebra, I trudged to the cafeteria for lunch. I met Missy at our mail boxes; we were both ecstatic that neither's box was empty. Our hunger for news and information, anything providing a fresh view of life other than textbooks, was as hearty as our appetites for food. I held back calling home as much as possible to keep the family phone bill under control. But I sure missed talking to my mother and even a note from home shot my spirits into the stratosphere. And now I even know where the stratosphere is, thanks to Astronomy.

My letter's from Purdue. A friend I knew since our high school freshmen days. And one who bragged about how many guys she could date simultaneously. I pocketed the letter for later. What my friend had to say, I didn't feel up to reading right now.

Missy's letter arrived from home. She opened it like a giddy child. God I hate that. Then again, that's how she acts most of the time. It's no wonder by the way she acts that she can't get a date.

My eyes alighted when the clerk handed me a package too large for my little box. Now *that* made up for my terrible morning and having to lunch without Duffy.

"You can reuse the stamps," the student postal worker said.

"What?"

"The stamps, if you can steam them off."

I stared at them.

"They're not cancelled," he added.

"Cookies!" Missy chimed, her tongue sliding along her lips. "I love your mother's chocolate chip brownies."

"Well I'll bet you do."

Now she's trying to make suck-up points. And that's even worse than her obnoxious giddy child routine.

The girls in my dorm named my mother Camp Pendleton Baking Queen. Her cookies went fast. They were always soft and chewy and packed solid with chocolate chips. They went so fast that I usually never got more than two.

Shuffling through the cafeteria line, I found myself wondering about Duffy. Was he putting me off? Did other interests really necessitate his cancellation? A pang struck my heart. I banished the thought that Duffy might be stringing me along for sex.

Rhonda waved from the farthest corner of the cafeteria to snare my attention. Her face blossomed into a smile when she spied the box on my tray.

"Here, sit next to me. Is that a care package I see," Rhonda said.

Missy and I settled across from Rhonda. The cafeteria noise seemed less intense in the corner. I then hung my backpack over the back of my chair and set the box prominently beside me on the table. It made me feel special. I had something they wanted.

"You're grinin' like a 'possum eatin' persimmons," Missy said in that way that gnaws at your patience.

I smiled, knowingly exactly what she meant.

People stared at my box as they passed. I felt a cut above them because my mother cared enough to send me a little bit of home.

"Trish got goodies from home," Rhonda whined, "All I ever get is a crummy letter and a lump of coal. Your mom's the best, my mom could learn a thing or two from her."

"Is that from Roger?" Missy asked, indicating the letter in Rhonda's hand.

"No, my mother. Roger, that lousy bum, hasn't written in over a week, I'm sure he'll try using one of his multitude of lame excuses like his pinkie finger on his writing hand was *sprained*," Rhonda sniped.

The grease-bucket cheeseburgers were cold and the french fries soggy. I wished now I would have gone for the fried catfish instead. However, the tidbits in the correspondence were hot and juicy.

My letter spanned a myriad of mundane details about school and academic pursuit, but with less than bubbling enthusiasm. I did learn that my friend had found a new man servant, as she called them, one that induced her to curtail her competitive dating practices. Ellen had once again been swept up into the ecstasy of really true love. Of course, Ellen habitually announced a short time thereafter that her prince had returned to being a bullfrog and the competition had once again resumed. I swear this girl goes through men faster than pantyhose.

I made a mental note to write Ellen about Duffy. Ten seconds later I reversed my thinking, deciding to hold off another week to see if we were still a couple. Seems I could never really be certain if Duffy was genuine or just stringing me along.

"So, you going to open it now?" Missy badgered. With lunch finished, I still made no motion for my box. I refused to even look at it and this agitated her even more.

"Probably not, she's waiting to share it with Dudley. You know, Dudley Do-right," Rhonda said, walking her fingers toward the box. She stopped them short and tapped them on the table in anticipation.

"I'll bet there's pecan nut brownies in there," Missy added. Even her sweetest Kentucky smile failed to move me.

"Look, I ate all my lunch...every bite. Now can I have some cookies? Please, oh please!" Rhonda begged the way a nine year old might.

"My Grandma Nizzie says..."

"We don't care!" both Rhonda and I blurted.

"Well, fine then."

"Okay, okay. I'll open it back at the room."

"Not fair. I've got a class," Rhonda brooded, urging me to end my toying.

"And his name is Duffy, not Dudley."

"Oh, touchy about old Dudley are we?"

I rose. My face hid the pleasure of my little game. I had something they wanted. Come to think of it, I also had Duffy. Something else I bet they wished they could have.

"Trish, remember you were asking around for girls who might have dated Delta Rho guys?"

"Yeah."

"I found one. A girl in my Biology class knows a girl who lived down the hall from a girl who dated a Delta Rho frat last year. She thinks she's back this year but doesn't know where she's living."

"Really!"

"Yeah. I got her name. You can look it up in the directory. I hope this helps."

"That's great. Anything will help."

"So, do I get a cookie?" Rhonda pleaded, handing over the paper.

"Oh, all right. Sit, I'll open it here. You each get two cookies before your next class."

I slit the tape sealing the flaps. The flaps rose. I closed them down.

"No, I should wait."

The din of conversations around us rose and fell like an ocean current.

"Fine. Your cookies are probably stale anyway!" Rhonda said, rising in a mock huff. She gathered her books and took a bold step away then spun back around and leaned across the table.

"Oh. please, please let me have a cookie," she begged as if her life hung in the balance.

I love when people grovel.

"Okay."

I opened the flaps. A white plastic bag filled the space with the top neatly tie-wrapped in the center.

"They're in plastic. They won't be stale!"

I untwisted the wire wrap. In exaggerated suspense, I pulled open the mouth of the bag peering inside.

My scream ripped through the cafeteria.

The room came to screeching silence. All eyes turned to our table in the corner.

I lurched away from the box and sent my chair reverberating to the floor.

Missy intervened to get a glimpse into the bag.

A brutally severed Calico cat's head, its rictus in a frozen snarl, stared back from the bag with clouded, vile eyes.

Missy slapped the box to the floor, rushing to grab me. I was quaking out of control. My face turned to bleached bone; my eyes were struck open in fright.

"Jesus Christ!" Rhonda yelled, seeing the bloody head roll from the box.

"Really frigging sick!" Missy stammered. She coaxed me away from the creature now half out of its plastic coffin and staring at us through those eyes as if it still had the power to see.

Blood splattered the tile floor and a horrid stench spread to the surrounding tables. Immediately, neighboring students fell under the foul odor and scrambled to evacuate. From the way everyone scattered, it must have looked like a brawl had broken out.

A black white-uniformed supervisor stormed the table; he must have thought that someone was injured. Instead, seeing the animal head on the floor, he kicked it back into the box, leaving behind a bloody splatter on the tiles. As he did, a creased slip of tainted paper appeared. In the next moment, box and beast were removed while students rushed to open windows.

There was no surrounding laughter as if it had been a prank. I scanned the faces. No one snickered privately to a friend when they realized what had happened. No eyes met mine in an exchange of recognition or warning.

Rhonda retrieved the paper, read it. Then she set it in my trembling hand.

This is what happens when a pussy sticks her nose where it doesn't belong!

As I held the note between weak fingers, my eyes moved over the words, though their meaning had yet to reach my brain.

Finally, Missy grabbed the paper from my hand, crumbled it into a ball and dumped it into a trash bin.

"Fucking creeps, that's what they are," she said.

I had never before heard Missy use profanity.

Rhonda and Missy walked me back to my room. Rhonda was going to miss her next class.

12

New Faces, New Hope

Hours passed. I lay motionless on my bed, staring at nothing. I tried Duffy. Still no answer. Whatever it was, something kept him out of his room all day.

Why was this happening to me? More importantly, who was terrorizing me?

I had no answers; yet I was convinced my probe into Ali's disappearance had struck a nerve. I shook off any doubts I might have harbored that Ali had come under foul deeds.

Somebody was trying damn hard to frighten me off. Somebody on campus knew exactly what happened to Ali and Matt.

I sat up in bed and stared out the window at a puffy afternoon sky. I wanted this to be a great year. I had set high goals and made a commitment to myself to see them through. Goals made inconsequential by Ali's disappearance.

Now my biggest worry was flunking out.

Why was someone working so hard to frighten me off? What did I know? The questions swirled through my mind like leaves churning in the breeze. What had I uncovered that put *them* in jeopardy? Was there even more than one person involved?

I stacked my gleanings like so many building blocks. Nothing pointed in a solid direction. Nothing offered me the slightest clue as to what had really happened to Ali.

So why was somebody using such tactics against me?

They must think I *have* something important. But what? Could I possibly be sitting on a vital clue without realizing it? After so long, was there still a chance of finding Ali...alive? Statistics painted a dismal picture for people missing more than forty-eight hours—they were either dead or gone forever. That thought sent a wave of anguish shuddering through me.

The note!

I frantically searched my desk. It wasn't there. I spun around, looking at my bed. Not there either. I plunged both hands into my pockets. I had to find that paper.

My Algebra book! Stuck inside was the slip of paper Rhonda had given me. I read the name aloud while pulling the directory from my drawer.

The phone rang four times before a cheerful voice answered.

"Hi-di-ho," she said.

"Can I speak with Elaine...Bal-icki," I asked.

"Sure, why not. You seem like a nice person. I can't come up with a single reason why you shouldn't be allowed to speak with Elaine."

A moment later Elaine came on.

"Hi, Elaine, Elaine Balicki?"

"Yes."

"I'm Patricia Van Worten. You don't know me, but I was wondering if I could talk with you for a minute?"

I buried my nervousness. This was as far as I had planned the conversation in my head.

"About what?"

"I understand you dated a Delta Rho frat last term," I said, plunging right in, my voice growing stronger.

"Yeah. So?"

"Well, are you aware Althea Goodfellow is missing?"

"No. And what has that got to do with me?"

"I was just hoping to talk to someone else who had gone out with a Delta Rho."

"The *Rho* (and she said it with such disdain) I dated was a shit-brained asshole. We broke up after a month. There's nothing to talk about. Good-bye."

I blurted a desperate plea, hoping for at least something; but before I could, the telephone went dead.

****

Between afternoon classes, I sat alone scouring Russian at a corner table in Charlie's. So consumed was I, that I never noticed Quenby standing at my table.

"Hi, Trish."

"Oh, hi Quenby, sorry. I'm behind and desperate. I have a Russian test next week."

"Then you would rather be alone?"

Disappointment crept into Quenby's words.

"No, yeah...if you wouldn't mind," I said with a stab at being assertive. Something I read somewhere. It rarely worked.

"I quite understand."

Quenby turned and feigned a search for another table.

"Wait. Why did you come by my room the other night?"

"Oh that, I..."

"Sit. I'll have time later," I said, closing my book.

"Right, okay," Quenby started, sitting across from me and setting his books down while masking a nervous twitch.

"About the other night. I...was, well, I thought...if you were alone, I'd come by your window, we could, you know, talk for a while."

"Really! That's nice. I would have liked that."

"Well, I could see something was going on inside your dorm, so I thought I'd go in and have a curious look see."

"Yeah, some friggin' asshole broke into my room."

"Did he get anything?"

"No money. That stays on me. Just my room-mate's jewelry case."

"I see."

Quenby sat in stilted silence, wishing he knew what to say to interest me but concerned that anything he said would come across clumsy. It was obvious to both of us that we were stuck in the middle of one of those awkward moments.

"So, you wanted to come by my window to talk?" I smiled.

"Yes. It was a pleasant night. And I always enjoyed just sitting outside talking to friends."

"You mean a girlfriend?"

"Yes, well actually, I was hoping to ask you for a date. But you were with what's his name, so I bowed out—as a gentleman should."

"Oh," I started. *Surprise!*

At our first meeting I was attracted to Quenby. He was cute, witty and very polite. Had he asked me out then, I would have accepted. However, now that I had met Duffy, I suddenly lost interest in Quenby, and Colin, and anybody else. Even Quenby's quaint British accent came up short next to Duffy. However, I did feel a stirring inside, but it rose out of Duffy's image painted on my mind.

"I'm sure this is awkward. I should let you get back to your studying."

"Wait, Quenby, I'm just interested in some-one else right now."

"I understand fully. We can still be friends, I hope?"

"Oh sure. You're a fun guy. You know any-thing about Algebra?"

"Sorry, can't help much there. Business major, you know. How about History? My passion is Medieval History."

While we talked, I pulled money from my pocket for the check. When I did, out came Ali's stone necklace. I set the stone on my book while I fingered my change.

"Where did you get that?" Quenby asked, suppressing a more-than-passing interest in the glistening jasper.

"It's Ali's. I must have stuck it in my pocket. I guess I forgot I had it."

I stopped, staring at the stone.

"I guess it's a good thing, or the thief might have taken it."

"Do you know what that is?"

"No. Isn't it weird. Look at the spiraling pattern and those three specks that reflect the light."

"I know. Trish, that isn't an ordinary stone," Quenby said, looking strangely into my eyes. "You ever hear of a Bloodstone?"

"No, why?"

"This looks like one. I think...I'm not completely certain, though. May I have a closer look?"

I offered it to him.

"Is it valuable?"

Quenby set the stone in his palm and draped the necklace through his fingers. The necklace material had an unusual feel that he must have detected because he inspected it closely.

"Well yes, but not in a way you might think. It's not worth a lot of money or anything like that."

"Then what makes it valuable?"

Quenby choked off his words. He feigned intense interest in the stone. The glistening pattern must have stirred up bits and pieces from deep in Quenby's academically cluttered memory.

"Well?"

"I'm sorry, what?"

"What makes it valuable?"

"Nothing, actually. I was thinking of something else."

Quenby's words faded. He returned the stone, his finger running along the smooth band.

"Maybe the chap who burgled your room was looking for this? Could Ali have gotten it from someone who wanted it back?"

"Beats me. Quenby, could that stone...never mind. I gotta go. And Quenby, you can come by my window any time you want."

"Smashing."

Quenby smiled, but his lips barely hid the workings of his mind. The moment I turned, out of corner of my eye, I saw his smile drop. He knew that stone was special.

13

The Wrong Place

Thursday night I found myself daydreaming on a third floor farmhouse widow's walk while I idled away the empty minutes waiting for my turn at one of the telescopes. The night breeze blew across my face and jostled my hair in an irritating way. I wished now I would have pulled my hair back to keep it out of my face. I never realized Astronomy could be such a dull subject.

I thought not about constellations or the moon, or Sociology or Algebra for that matter, but rather what was happening to my secure, controlled world. I found little impetus now to sustain my drive to locate Ali. As each day passed, I felt my grip weakening. Ali was gone. For whatever reason. I had to face that. I might never see her again. So why was it so hard to get myself back together and go on? If I remained passive, this would be my last semester at Ranhurst.

A nudge from my lab partner returned me to the soft glow of the overhead moon. The clear night sky offered students a spectacular laboratory for their assigned exercises. No sooner had I settled in behind a telescope, when the postgraduate lab assistant called an end to the session. What a terrible way to spend an evening. But I needed the science credit and thought Astronomy would be an easy course. *Not!*

I filed onto the bus for the return to the campus. A handful of cars roared out of the makeshift gravel parking lot. I noticed that most of the students had left earlier. Only a handful remained to ride the bus back. Everyone hated night lab sessions. Nights were for partying, or studying, in my case.

Ten minutes later the bus rolled to a squealing stop before Administration, and one by one the students piled off. Before long I was alone on the lighted path meandering through the western corner of Ranhurst. In the distance, the twisting concrete spilled onto Main Street two blocks before Camp Pendleton.

A trio of students passed. Once their voices faded, I realized the depth of my solitude.

Shouldering my backpack, I quickened my stride. As I walked, I rummaged through my pack and pulled out my tape player. I then blindly felt along the bottom until I found my favorite tape. But I stopped short of slipping the tape into the player.

A fleeting shadow on the fringes of my vision snared my attention. Oh God, I'm not alone. A change in the umbra—an apparition—registered in my brain.

I stared straight ahead and quickened my pace.

Overhead, halogen lamps dropped light cones onto the walkway. However, the distance between stanchions left vast expanses of pitch. Areas I had to pass through.

My heartbeat quickened. I tightened a fist on my pack, foregoing music. The surrounding night sent icy chills up my spine. I was hoping it was just my imagination toying with my brain. But in the next moment I spied the shadow again and knew this was real.

Snap!

The sound of a breaking limb came in my wake.

I spun around in unmasked fear. Terror seized my lungs. I was still alone on the walkway.

Far away voices filtered through the trees. Somewhere people were laughing. Then a car with a loud muffler roared past.

A body flowed in my wake, clinging to the trees on my left. The umbra's changing hues reflected movement.

I slowed as terror knotted my heart and choked off my throat. My mouth dried...swallowing became impossible.

There! Another. A black outline on my right. More than one.

I scanned my left.

Nothing.

Instinct kicked in. I broke into a run.

But confusion reigned. Which way? Where were they? They slithered through the darkness like snakes safe beneath the grass. I heard sounds. They were stalking me, moving on a parallel course at the same pace.

Suddenly pounding footfalls.

I exploded into full pelt. I slid my bag into my hand to be used as a weapon. Without thinking, I whirled, swinging the backpack at arm's length. My pack flew into the depths of the darkness.

My pounding feet outraced my frantic heart. Tears threatened sight. I commanded a scream, yet had not the force to release the volcanic eruption of terror inside.

A flurry of motion in a nearby thicket told me they were closing fast like animals in pursuit of prey.

"Oh God," I found the strength to cry out.

Then came angry yells, not words; they were homing in.

A black faceless human mass skulked out from a grove.

I left the path for the safety of the trees. Defenseless, I dug in my toes and ran with all my strength.

An arm shot out from behind a tree to snag my flowing hair. I was forced about, facing a black mask with dark eyes. Behind my eyes the green specks arose. Everything became blurry and the color of mint leaves.

Searing pain wrenched my chest. In that terrifying moment it was like I became suspended— no longer in control of my body or my mind. It was as if I suddenly became a spectator of my own life.

"*This bitch is mine!*" I heard a foul guttural voice inside me issue. Everything wavered in and out of focus. I knew my arms and legs were thrashing.

A bone snapped! An blood-curdling scream flooded my head.

I was free, in control again, and running.

I mustered the strength to scream. Other pounding feet grew closer. My lungs wanted to burst. Why was no one coming to help me?

Then more groans of agony from behind—a sudden tumult of terrible pain.

The night fell silent. The footfalls vanished.

My lungs were like stretched balloons, threatening to explode. Fire burned my chest, crawling up the back of my throat. I had to stop. Tears all but stole away my vision. I couldn't stop.

Ahead, prismatic lines of the street lamps spilled onto the walkway. Main Street. The trees receded to form a gateway. I sucked in air.

Reaching the welcome openness of the street, I slowed, stealing a glance over my shoulder. The walkway was as quiescent as the night. Whoever they were—they were gone now.

A boisterous gang crossed Clinton Avenue heading for the walkway. I buried my panic, wiping my eyes while forcing cool air deep into my lungs.

A metallic blue Mustang that matched the night slowed in passing. Rock music gyrations pumped out the open windows with so much pulsating bass that anyone within ten feet felt it.

Inside, a very interested face leaned forward for a closer look at me.

I immediately came about, blending in with the group. The car, forced to increase speed by approaching headlights, faded from sight.

Who was after me? More importantly, why were they after me? Was the Mustang in league with those on the walkway?

14

Look Everywhere

Trembling fingers locked the door. Inside I was safe. Or was I?

I quaffed down the only thing in the refrigerator to drink—a can of Ali's Mountain Dew—wishing it had an alcoholic potency to settle my nerves. What was happening?

For five long minutes I curled in the darkened corner of my bed. I was hidden, if only scantily, from the terrors of the outside world. My heart finally returned to the rhythm of the sane. I felt in control again.

I dialed the phone praying they would be there to answer it.

My mother picked up after the third ring. Her voice was wonderful beyond belief. Our conversation lasted most of an hour. Throughout the exchange I remained cheery, burying the horror of the incident down so deep it could never creep into my voice.

School's fine. Yes, I'm studying hard. No, I'm eating three meals a day in the cafeteria and avoiding junk food.

Inside I was terrified. I wanted to cry. While my hands trembled, my voice remained level, almost casual.

I met a great guy and, yes, we're dating. More than one date. No, he's a perfect gentleman.

If only my mother knew how much her words were helping at this moment. My inner voice urged to me to reveal everything that had happened. Another voice warned against it.

It was crazy to keep this from my parents. They should know what I had faced just an hour ago. But I knew if I said anything, my parents would yank me out of Ranhurst in a snap. If they learned of Ali's disappearance, the vandal invading my room, and now the…. No, it was time to say good-bye. I promised to call again next week. Hanging up, I sought to face my world anew. I had to fortify my courage and push forward. Someone doesn't want me looking for Ali. That's got to mean Ali is still to be found. Whether dead or alive, I could only pray she would still be alive. But I had to keep pushing.

Sleep crowded the fringes of my mind. In its stead, I recounted every detail of every incident that transpired since arriving at Ranhurst.

Ali disappears.

The strange stone in Ali's clothes.

Someone breaks into our room.

The gruesome warning in the cafeteria.

Stalkers attack me in the night.

Then my subconscious, a part of me that had been fondling the shards of information, began to slowly arrange them into a cogent picture.

I thought about the Bloodstone. Could that be what they wanted? I removed the stone from around my neck to study it. Was this what they were really after?

If Ali just took off, why were these things happening to me? In a moment I knew why.

I was the only one questioning Ali's disappearance. I probed and prodded like a doctor seeking to uncover the source of a patient's complaint. And I must have hit a nerve, causing the patient to recoil. I was trying to find Ali. And somebody doesn't want Ali found.

Whoever is involved in Ali's disappearance is keeping an eye on me, trying to frighten me off. The stone may have nothing to do with it.

I bolted up in bed. Had they intended on raping me?

The phone rang. I let it ring. I needed solitude right now. Should I tell Duffy? Should I tell Merrifield?

****

I slumped over breakfast, weighed down with the lethargy of a sleepless night. I picked at watery scrambled eggs and carbon toast. College food...there's no place like home!

Rhonda had just said something, and when I offered no response, she repeated it. Still, it was all a jumble in my head.

I looked up with zero comprehension in my eyes, like I did most of the time in Algebra. I shrugged, then pushed my eggs away.

"Hi. That looks good," a much-too-cheery voice said from behind me.

I jumped.

Duffy sat down beside me, presuming an invitation. He set my backpack on the table as if he were displaying a trophy or something.

"Found it on the way over. Thought I'd take a chance and see if you were still around."

"You found this?"

"Yeah, over by Reynolds Hall."

I smiled vacantly like I had no explanation.

Duffy pointed politely to a piece of black-fringed toast.

Missy contributed her untouched orange juice.

"This stuff is flavored water compared to the Donald Duck juice I get back home," she said.

"What? What did you say?"

"Listen, if you're only going put me down, I'm just going to get up and leave."

"No. I mean you said Donald Duck orange juice."

"Yeah, don't you have it in Chicago?"

"No."

"So, why are you so interested in it now?"

"I don't know," I said.

Donald Duck orange juice. Why did that trigger something in my brain? I tossed the words back and forth inside my head until I had to abandon them for lack of recognition. If only I could figure out why that seemed important to me.

"This stuff is really good. You should try this," Duffy said packing his mouth like a squirrel at the onset of winter. He had to be the only student at Ranhurst who actually enjoyed the food. And there is definitely something wrong with a person who relishes cafeteria food.

"So, you want to tell me?" he asked a moment after swallowing, and against the silence when no explanation seemed forthcoming.

Rhonda eyes bounced curiously between me, Duffy and the backpack.

"Tell you what?"

"Oh, how your Astronomy book, lab notes and tape player ended up in the bushes between here and Reynolds Hall."

"No."

"Okay, don't tell me if you don't want to."

I renewed the silence at the table. One by one the other girls drifted away.

Once alone, I stared into Duffy's eyes.

He recognized fear. Real serious fear. The kind of fear that is life threatening. His hand came over to cover mine in reassurance.

"Someone came after me last night." My voice faltered.

Duffy stared.

"Were you alone?"

"Yes. I was walking back from the observatory bus."

"No one else got off the bus?"

"Yes. Will you please listen. The other students took other routes. I don't know. Before long I was alone on the walkway. I heard noises in the trees. Then I saw one, no, two silhouettes. They were in black or something like that. I couldn't see anything but faint outlines. Duffy, there were at least *two* of them lying in wait for me."

"Are you sure? You sound paranoid."

"Duffy, I'm frigging scared. The campus police aren't doing a damn thing to locate Ali. And every time I ask questions, I have to look over my shoulder. Something is going on. Ali's involved, I know it for sure now."

"Ali could be long gone by now."

"So if Ali's gone, why is someone trying so hard to get to me?"

"I don't know. You going to Merrifield with this?"

"Yeah, right. I don't trust him either."

"What are you going to do?"

"I don't know yet. I keep wondering if Ali is an innocent victim, or if she's somehow tied into whatever is happening?"

"You're getting in way over your head. Why don't you just let the police handle this thing."

"Oh sure, they spent ten minutes in the room, did a half-assed search of the woods, and now they're convinced Ali just ran away."

"Okay, fine. If you're right, this could get dangerous. I think you should back off, let the authorities handle it."

In the ensuing silence, I inventoried my backpack.

"I still think Delta Rho is involved. I don't know how yet, but I'm going to damn well find out."

I rose with rock-solid determination. I intended to continue my own investigation.

Duffy shot a hand up to snare my arm.

"Promise me one thing."

"What?"

"Call me whenever you're going to be out after dark, and you never go anywhere by yourself."

"What am I, a kid? There's a college full of people here."

"Patricia Lynn, I'm serious. I'll walk you anywhere you have to go. I don't want you out by yourself. Call me if you need a ride. I'll borrow my roommate's car. Understand?"

"Patricia Lynn? How did you get my middle name?"

"I have my sources in Administration."

"Duffy, your nose is finally back to normal. And I happen to like your face just the way it is. I'm not so sure you really want to do this."

I kissed him on impulse. His lips were warm and reassuring.

"Trust me. I really want to do this. Now promise. If I'm unavailable, call the campus escort service. They'll have someone see you safely to your destination."

I promised only after Duffy refused to release my hand until I did. A hesitation in my voice sharpened Duffy's concern. After I promised, Duffy took my other hand.

I held on tight.

****

The afternoon air was hot and sticky, the sky cloudless. I left my last class of the day and trudged back to my dorm suffering from an exhausting case of brain strain. Mathematics boggled my mind. I knew it and hated the fact that something so logical could make me feel so inadequate. If it's so logical, why is it so hard?

As I strolled, I rid my mind of those ridiculous, obnoxious variables.

Shrill laughter charged the air. The girls were in the pits between buildings bantering a volleyball back and forth with more zeal than they devoted to their studies.

Too hot, I thought. All I wanted was to kick off my shoes and sit in front of the fan.

For the first time that day, swirling uncertainties about Ali spilled into my mind. So entrenched in thought was I, that I never perceived the slow rider approaching from behind.

I lurched out of the way at the last second as Catwoman peddled by, wiping sweat from her eyes and trying to control her handle bars. She veered at the last moment but too late to avoid me.

The handle bar cracked into my elbow and sent searing pain through my entire arm.

Catwoman stopped and turned her head in a creepy birdish fashion. The sweat-stained cowboy hat shaded Catwoman's dark, staring eyes.

Did she intentionally hit me?

"Hey, watch where the hell you're going!" I scowled.

"Sorry. I came too close. I wasn't watching, I'm sorry," Catwoman apologized with adolescent sincerity. She offered a gap-toothed smile that forced her eyes nearly closed.

"Well, I'd appreciate it if you'd just stay the goddamn hell off the sidewalks. Ride your damn bike in the streets."

"I said I'm sorry. I can only say I'm sorry. I was just searching for my cat. She's missing, you know. I've looked..."

"Yeah, I know, Catwoman," I blurted coldly, hoping to force Catwoman to abort the conversation.

Catwoman's darting eyes grew sullen. She despised the name *we* had forced upon her. She had done nothing deserving of our ridicule and loathing.

Catwoman locked her stare on me. Something in her sad eyes urged me to abandon my stern facade.

In that moment, I saw a glint of recognition—something quite incomprehensible. Sweat trickled down Catwoman's pallid cheeks. Her dark facial hair painted a hint of a moustache. The quizzical look almost induced me to apologize for my outburst. Almost.

"When you lose something, something important, you must try to find it. You understand? *You* must try to find it," Catwoman repeated innocently.

"Yeah, right Catwoman. How about..."

"You know what I mean, you do."

Catwoman said no more. She pushed off, struggled during the first revolution of her peddles, then glided away, never looking back.

I stood there, lost in the crazy woman's words. What did she mean?

"You must look everywhere to find what you have lost," came from Catwoman as a whisper on the wind.

I gotta be losing my mind. Why is this happening?

It wasn't until I had dropped my books on my desk, kicked my shoes under the chair, and turned my fan on high that I began to replay Catwoman's words.

Could she somehow know Ali is missing? Was she attempting in her own way to tell me something? Or was I now reading intrigue into everything I heard?

"What happened Ali? Where are you? Tell me how to help you!" I asked my empty room.

15

Somebody Else Cares

"Duffy's House of Pleasure," Duffy said in response to my ring.

"I just got a call from somebody who says he may have information about Ali."

I was breathless.

"I'm on my way."

"Duffy, wait!" I screamed into the line, "I have to leave right now. I'm meeting him at the library."

"The library. That's just as far as Camp Pendleton. It will take me twenty minutes, even if I run. Trish, stay where you are. I'll be right over."

"I can't. I'm leaving right now. Meet me there."

"Listen...." Duffy yelled into the phone; he got an earful of dial tone.

I arrived at the library, my heart racing, my breathing a bellow. I had run most of the way, slowing to a walk only when my lungs burned.

Browsing through a card catalog for a minute, I scanned the surrounding tables. No one demonstrated more than a passing interest in me. No eyes locked on mine in some clandestine signal of recognition. Could one of them be the caller? What information could he have?

I jotted down some meaningless numbers. With clinched jaw and constantly roving eyes, I began an earnest quest for a book.

The voice had definitely been male, somewhat uncertain, and abrupt. I cautioned myself to be prepared for anything.

Eyes rose over books or around newspapers to notice me as I moved down the aisles. The caller provided very specific instructions, which I now followed explicitly.

Scratching my head in mock confusion, I descended to the lower level. Once amid the shelves, I glanced to a door on an outside wall with a squarely affixed sign that read, 'NO STUDENT ACCESS.'

I glanced back up the stairs. A Bleat with dreadlocks descended slowly toward me. I cast my eyes askance when he looked at me. He passed, turning down the second aisle on the left.

I stalled, picking a book off a shelf while a group of chattering girls walked past. My eyes rose to the door. One final check—no one in sight.

I set the book on the shelf, slipped through the unlocked door and eased it closed.

Once inside, I flapped my hand along the wall until I flicked on the lights. Pulsating florescents settled upon a cluttered, little-used storage room filled with old newspapers, blueprints and damaged books.

Stacks of discolored newspapers filled a long trestle table, with the overflow heaped on the floor beside it. I crossed to the table and ran my fingers over some yellowed pages spread out on the surface. Newspaper sheets from fifty years ago.

The door opened.

I came about, clutching my chest.

A black security officer with an empty, cold stare filled the doorway. Tanner. The one I had spoken to on my first visit to campus security.

"You're not supposed to be in here. Can't you read?"

"I..."

Before I could deliver my ill-conceived response, the platyrrhine-faced guard gently closed the door behind him.

I swallowed hard when the lock clicked; his dark eyes all the while remained fixed on me.

I backed into the table.

"You the one looking for Althea Goodfellow?" he asked.

I recognized the voice.

"Yes, you know something?"

"Maybe."

We stared at each other for a moment.

"First, your word you ain't gonna reveal where you got this, or that you even know about it."

It wasn't a request. It was a demand.

"Promise."

He studied my eyes as if he could see inside to scrutinize my honor. The moment hung between us.

I felt the sweat rolling down my neck.

The guard's swift movement broke the stillness.

I flinched.

He eased past me to a rusted green filing cabinet. Kneeling down, he reached behind it. A second later he came up with a crumbled paper bag.

"Look at this." He shoved a rectangular weighty object onto my open palm.

I peeled back the bag, my face wrought in confusion. I lifted out a yellow, weather-beaten Sports Walkman.

"Could that belong to the girl?" the guard queried. His serious eyes locked onto mine.

"I don't know. Ali has a tape player, I know that much, but I don't know what kind it is."

I examined it more closely. Sony. It could have been Ali's—it could have been anyone's.

"No initials or markings on it?"

"Nothing."

"Why do you think this might have something to do with Ali?"

The guard took the player from me, re-examined it.

"Call it a hunch. Merrifield was real interested in it when he learned we found it in a thicket."

"Yeah so?"

"So, Merrifield locked it away. At the same time, he dismissed it as meaningless."

I shook my head in confusion.

"If it's so damn meaningless, why was *he* so interested?"

I took it back, anxious now to see something that may well not be there.

"Nobody knows I've got it. Merrifield's jumpy, unsure of himself. People are asking questions. Questions make Merrifield nervous. This is his college. He doesn't like people nosing around."

I shook my head. Still nothing.

"Thought maybe you might know if this belongs to the missing girl."

"I don't know what kind of player she had."

"I have to get it back before Merrifield realizes its gone. I was hoping it might mean something to you. Between you and me, that girl's disappearance ain't no quirk. There's some weird shit going on 'round here. People are nervous. I see it in the way they act."

I studied the player again. A moment later I abandoned my examination. I extended my arm to hand it back to the guard, but I stopped short. I pulled open the door. A water-damaged tape was still in it. Sawyer Brown. That name meant something to me, but what?

"Sorry. I know you've been pushing Merrifield to find out what happened to the girl," the officer said. His voice held an edge of disappointment. "Just thought you might want to know what we found."

"I do, thanks, I really do appreciate this," I said absently.

Even as I spoke, my mind raced back over the past week. The lock's click drew me out of my thoughts.

"Where did you find it?" I asked in a rush, before the guard opened the door.

"In some bushes, about ten yards north of Chandler Hall. Do me a favor. Let me leave the building before you. I don't want people seeing us together."

I nodded. I wanted to say more, but only thanked him instead.

"Don't be a bit surprised if this Walkman walks off," he said.

The guard was gone.

I remained in the room long after the door closed. Fragments raced through my mind, too fast to catch. In those hazy moments, I realized there was only one way to know if what I had seen was important.

Driven by the urge to get back to my room, I opened the storage room door. I stuck my head out just enough to be sure my departure would pass unnoticed. Then I slid out, closing the door behind me.

"Hey!" a voice called from behind me.

I jumped, whirling around to square off against the voice.

"It's me," Duffy said, taking my arms, "I've been looking all over for you. Damnit, I told you to wait! I..."

Duffy's dripping face was writ with concern. Anger tainted his words. His wet hair clung to his forehead.

All eyes shifted to me and Duffy.

I ripped free of his grip.

"You don't own me. Don't tell me what to do!"

I raced up the stairs, past the crowded checkout desk and through the doors.

Rain pelted my face as I padded down the slick stone steps, my hand clinging to the cold handrail for balance.

A dozen strides later, as I splashed through a puddle, Duffy reached out to snare me out of my flight.

I swung about, my angry eyes flashing into his.

"I'm sorry," he yelled above the roar of the driving rain. He scooped my trembling body against my will into his arms. Duffy never saw the tears coalescing with the rain streaming down my cheeks.

"I'm sorry, I just care about you. I lov..." Duffy stopped, realizing his emotions were flowing as freely as the cloud burst overhead.

"You what?"

"I'm concerned about you."

"That's not what you sai..."

Duffy silenced me with a kiss.

I offered no resistance. I released myself completely to him as he wrapped his warmth around me. He held me close, feeling my warm trembling lips against his, my body pressed against his shivering frame.

Rain ran down our faces.

"I said I love you! I don't want anything to happen to you."

Now my tears became undeniable.

"I'm sorry, Trish," he said again as if he needed some sign of forgiveness from me. Our hands remained locked. Duffy waited.

I answered him with another kiss.

"Let's get out of this rain!" I yelled.

Twenty minutes later, while rain tapped at the window, Duffy and I stood dripping in the warm confines of my room. Music from a triad of stereos played in the background. Water puddled beneath our feet, but we never moved to step out of it.

Duffy held my hands, kissing me gently, afraid that if he released me, I might be spirited away from him forever.

"I think we need to dry off," I said, signaling I needed my hand back, even if only for a moment.

Duffy reluctantly released.

A raucous screaming laugh rose over the music. Duffy turned toward the door, expecting one of the girls to come banging on it any second. Please, let nothing destroy this moment, I thought.

I tossed him a towel, hitting him in the head when he turned back toward me. My smile was unreadable while I toweled my soaked hair.

After drying off some, Duffy looped his towel over my head and eased me to him. He kissed me, shivering in his dripping clothes. When our lips parted, he turned his head away to sneeze.

"I think we're going to have to get out of these wet things before we both get sick," I said.

Duffy let the towel slip from his hand. Disappointment loomed in his eyes. He wanted to stay; he wanted to know if he had made a fool of himself. However, he understood the implication in my statement.

He had opened up his heart. Yet having done so, I offered no acknowledgment. I never once revealed how I felt about him. I must feel different, Duffy must think, standing before me.

"I'll call you tomorrow," he offered.

The dorm had grown quiet around us. Duffy rubbed the towel quickly through his hair, then set it over the back of Ali's chair. It was late. Maybe it was better to go.

Before Duffy could reach the door, I slipped around him and turned the lock. With my back still to him, I flipped off the light.

"I think I love you too, Duffy," I whispered so that only he would hear.

****

The dorm began coming to life at seven. Scantily robed girls padded up and down the hall in urgent pursuit of a shower or a blouse.

This morning, however, I lingered in bed, warm and cozy beneath my blanket. I savored my memory of being in Duffy's arms. I hadn't slept this well since leaving home. Duffy had been here beside me, had left me with a kiss when it was time to leave. Now I was alone, reliving the intimacy we had shared.

My night had all the fabric of a fairy tale come true. Duffy had been gentle and caring. I never knew love could feel this wonderful. There was no groping, no pressure. This was the first time I had felt this kind of love. I felt it—truly felt it—inside.

The boundaries I set, he accepted without retort. Instead of pressure, instead of pushing to find my limit, in a soft whisper so endearing it will forever remain in my memory, he said he would wait for me until the fading glimmer of the last sunset.

I checked the clock. Maybe I would skip my first class, hang on to this moment as long as I could. Maybe not. If I missed Abernathy's lecture, I would probably flunk his exam.

With a sudden fury, I bolted up in my bed.

The tape!

I had forgotten about the cassette tape.

I stumbled out of bed to Ali's desk. There in the drawers were the same six cassette tapes I had seen on my first weekend back. I remembered returning them to the drawer after the break-in.

Something was missing. Something wasn't here. It wasn't anywhere. I rifled through the side drawers, shuffling through odds and ends frantically. It wasn't here.

Like a caged animal, I paced back and forth. What was it that had seized my attention? Why did I have to go through Ali's things?

"Think, damnit!"

In angry frustration, I returned to the middle drawer of Ali's desk. This time I worked my way methodically through each item. In my haste I had tossed things back in, paying little attention to what filled the space.

In the very back of the drawer, lodged behind a small book on word usage, I withdrew another cassette case.

Sawyer Brown!

I opened it—empty. The tape was gone.

The tape in the Walkman was Sawyer Brown. The Walkman the security officer said they found near Chandler Hall. The one he thought might have something to do with Ali's disappearance.

I searched each desk drawer thoroughly. An excitement rushed through me as I finished the last drawer. I had confirmed it. The tape that belonged inside that particular case was nowhere in the room. That was because Ali had taken *that* tape to listen to when she left the room that Friday.

"It *was* Ali's Walkman!" I shouted to the room.

I called Duffy.

Duffy was still asleep as he spoke into the mouthpiece.

I spoke so fast, and my voice was so fraught with excitement, that most of what I said made no sense at all.

"What are you saying?" Duffy asked, now more awake.

"I'm saying I saw Ali's Walkman!"

"Are you sure? I mean are you really sure?"

Duffy was suddenly alert.

"Positive. The tape in the Walkman was Sawyer Brown."

"So?"

"So, there's an empty Sawyer Brown case in Ali's desk."

"So."

"It means Ali lost it near Chandler Hall. It means Ali was near Chandler Hall after arriving back at Ranhurst? It could mean..."

"Trish, it could mean almost anything. Isn't that what they call circumstantial?"

"Duffy, Sawyer Brown is country. How many country fans do you think are on this campus?"

"More than just Ali."

Duffy said he had to go, he was late for class.

I held the receiver long after his voice faded.

16

Spreading The Good Word

Missy and I arranged to meet outside the humanities building after my Russian class. We could walk over to Administration together, since each had an appointment with our respective counselors around the same time.

I needed to talk seriously about my graduation requirements; I may need to take on a heavier load next semester to make a four year graduation. My father would throw fits if I had to become a 'fifth year' senior; and Missy needed to begin her search for a law school. With her grades she believed she could have her pick of the best. I just couldn't see Missy as a hard driving ruthless lawyer. If anyone were meant to be Suzy Homemaker it was Missy.

Missy sat on the stone ledge waiting. I was already twenty minutes late. If I failed to show in two minutes, Missy would have to go on alone. I thought about abandoning the rendezvous and heading over to Administration on my own.

"Isn't this a wonderful Lord's day," a voice behind me said as I approached the stone steps.

Missy slid to her feet and shifted her books, anxious for me to arrive.

"Sorry I'm late," I said trudging up.

"Have you accepted Jesus Christ as your Lord and Savior?" Jacob asked me.

I guess some people can't understand that if you refuse to acknowledge them that means you don't wish to talk to them. This guy was having a thinking problem.

"No I haven't, and gee, look at the time. Well, I gotta go. We're late for appointments."

"Trish wait," Missy started.

Jacob took my hand.

For a moment I hesitated. He seemed to be some strange guy who just showed up on campus this year. Probably not even a real Christian. There were a flood of stories about guys using religion to seduce naive young girls on campus. Yet his gentle touch had a way of putting you at ease. Suddenly he didn't seem like such a bad person.

"It only takes a moment to meet Jesus Christ."

"Oh, is he around?" I said sardonically.

"He is everywhere."

I surrendered my hand fully to Jacob just wanting to get it over with. Maybe if I give him his two minutes, he'll leave me alone and I can go on with my life. Why do these religious fanatics have to be so pushy when it comes to religion anyway? Each religion thinks theirs is the true faith and only their road leads to paradise. Yeah sure.

Jacob held my hand tight, but still loose enough that I could remove it if I really wanted. His smile and eyes were soft, gentle and sincere. His warmth put me at ease.

"We are all lost until we find Jesus Christ." His eyes peered into mine.

"This is really great, but I do have an appointment."

"The only appointment you dare not miss is the one with our Lord, here, today."

Jacob's words flowed like honey. His touch melted away my apprehension. For a brief moment, I actually felt as if he were reaching me. Then Jacob's eyes drifted down, not in any lecherous way, just naturally. Here it comes, creepo here thinks his going to show me the way and in the process have my body for his efforts. His eyes settled upon the stone between my breasts. As he stared at it, his eyes became cold and distant.

I felt my hand tightening on his. Yet I was doing nothing to constrict it. Every muscle in my body became frozen. I wanted to release his hand and leave, yet I became incapable of doing anything. Then....

Jacob tugged gently to ease his hand out.

I mashed his knuckles like a vise. His eyes grew wide; not with anger but with terror, as if something horrifying had taken over. I commanded myself to release him. Something inside disobeyed. I felt some kind of strange power swarming over me. Regardless of what I commanded, I became impotent to execute my desires.

My face moved intimately close to Jacob's ear. I could smell his sweat and feel his trembling through our contact.

"I'll be fucking you in hell," that strident alien voice inside of me whispered. Did I say the words or just imagine them? Jacob recoiled. I must have said them.

"You are evil," Jacob snapped, his voice growing cold and driving. He ripped his hand free of mine.

I smiled with a diabolic glint. Then it was gone. I turned my back on Jacob and marched down the steps. I dared not look back.

"Seek Jesus now, turn away before it is too late. Only he can free you from the evil one."

Jacob's voice rose to a frantic pitch as he backed away from me.

Something inside me forced me about to home in on his eyes. It was like something was using my eyes to get one final look at Jacob.

Even a concerned Missy edged away.

"Never give yourself to him," Jacob persisted from an expanding distance.

"What did you say to him?" Missy asked as we hurried on our way.

I offered a look of genuine confusion.

"Nothing."

Missy looked back at the fleeing Jacob.

"Thank you heaps and noodles, Missy," I said after glancing back to make sure Jacob no longer pursued us. Now moments afterward, if you asked me just what happened back there, I'd be at a lose to explain it.

"I'm sorry, Trish. How was I to know he'd get weird. I just thought it wouldn't hurt if he talked to you about God."

"Thanks, but no thanks. You have your religion and that's great for you. But it's not for me. I'll find my own faith in my own time, okay?"

"Okay. But there is just so much evil out there. The Devil doesn't care how he gets you as long as he gets you! You know what they say: he'll use an ocean of truth to hide an ounce of lie."

"What are you talking about Missy?"

"Well, in Bible Study, we saw a video about how they put stuff in album covers and how they steal peoples' pets and sacrifice them, and it's happening everywhere, all over the world.... And with that cat and all..."

"Oh, come on, Missy, you need to get out more and not just to Bible Studies. I'll probably find you out there preaching one day soon."

Missy shut up and sulked the rest of the day. She did however, continue to mumble something about the devil appearing as a beautiful angel of light.

17

Sweet Dreams, My Little One

By the pile of clothes heaped on Ali's bed, I realized laundry day had come and gone unattended to. Actually, I had exhausted my supply of clean clothes and could forestall the inevitable no longer.

My father said there were two things certain in life: death and taxes. Mother added dirty laundry.

I hated laundry. I knew I would never become that sickly-sweet, apron-bound housewife so many women longed to be. That was the kind of life destined for Missy and Rhonda. Not me. I had more important things to accomplish in my life. I realized I hadn't given Ali's disappearance a thought all day.

Twice in as many days I went through my clothes pile, hoping to pull out something wearable one more time before the moment of dread arrived. Not that I made it a habit of dressing laundry-bag fashion. I had just let myself get lazy, and between classes and trying to come up with the next step in investigating Ali's disappearance, I just had no time for anything else.

But now the chore became unavoidable. So, changing into volleyball shorts and t-shirt, I trudged to the washeteria with quarters in one hand and clothes bag in the other. I had stuffed every garment I owned into my bag, save for that one formal dress in my closet reserved for that elusive special occasion.

The washeteria machines chugged pleasantly away, though no one sat in attendance. I set my sack down on the vibrating lid of a noisy machine then began pulling out my things. Responding to a mother's conditioning, I checked all pockets, making certain I retrieved my ID card and any money before they went into the wash with the clothes.

Of course, money at college was a scarce commodity. My weekly allowance long overdue, I would rejoice if I were lucky enough to find even a single bill inside any of my pockets. Just enough for a small pizza supreme with double pepperoni. No such luck. And I was already into

Rhonda over my limit, so I just had to rough it until that ten spot arrived from home.

Curling my fingers in the last pocket, and abandoning all hope of gaining any cash in this endeavor, I removed the Bloodstone.

Under the washeteria's flickering fluorescents, the stone had lost some luster, but the three specks still captured my eyes.

Doling out the required quarters, the stone became a nuisance. As a result, I slipped the necklace on, allowing the stone to fall beneath my shirt.

Movement along my periphery snared me. He seemed to walk out of the night to enter the washeteria. I froze. My stomach constricted, backing bitter bile into my throat. My mind raced to find a way out of this place. His hair was spiked and cranberry-colored. His acne-infested face made his ominous. He stopped a dozen paces from me and just stared.

I balled my hands into fists.

Then he turned to a machine, lifted the lid and began drawing out stings of dark clothing.

I began to breath again.

My machine filled with a hiss. Nothing left now but to wait. But I wasn't going to wait around here. Though the guy never looked at me again, I decided it was best to put distance between us. Besides, I still had a ton of work to do and nothing productive was getting done standing here watching the clothes in the dryers tumble.

I wished Duffy had been home when I tried him earlier. This was a time we could spend together. But Duffy was out and his roommate had no idea when he would be back.

Great.

My books awaited me anyway. I could postpone destiny no longer.

Back in my room, I sat over my books, my mind as uncluttered as my surroundings. My eyes saw the words, but nothing stuck inside my brain. Though I faithfully worked through an Astronomy exercise, I felt I had attained no greater cosmic knowledge. For a fleeting moment I thought I understood the exercise, but now, having completed it, I sat in mind-boggling confusion.

Like an angered evil queen, I banished my Astronomy book to the furthest corner of my desk. Punishment for its unreasonable demeanor. I'll teach it a lesson it'll never forget.

Glancing at the clock, I realized my machine had finished more than an hour ago. I rushed to the laundry room and suffered a tinge of fear when I noticed a lone male student sitting near my machine thumbing through a magazine. He had shaved the sides of his head up to the crown and fashioned the long hair remaining on top into a shoulder-length ponytail. Weird. His sunken eyes and scraggly goatee gave him a demonic visage.

Should I return later?

A few deep breathes and a quick scolding about irrational fears helped me overcome my paranoia. I strolled coolly over to my machine, confident and ready to go for the eyes and the groin at the first sign of attack, and I transferred my clothes to a dryer against the wall and never once acknowledged the guy.

He never looked up from his reading.

Even before I left the laundry room, I felt a sudden unexplainable exhaustion suck the life out of me. It seeped quickly into my limbs, rising like a toxic cloud to fill my head. It was too early for this. Shake it off, I told myself like a coach spurring on his best athlete. I still had hours of work to do.

Back in my room as I read, my eyes fluttered out of focus. My mind became a nag over my growing fatigue. The urge to curl beneath my blanket while I read constantly bantered my concentration. But I knew if I laid down now, I would fall fast asleep.

Inside, a voice prodded me to close the book.

I did.

It instructed me to turn off the study lamp.

I complied.

Finally, it demanded that I crawl into bed.

My clothes! If I went to bed now, my clothes would end up in a wrinkled ball in the corner of the washeteria.

That persistent voice urged me to abandon my clothes.

No way.

Each step back to the laundry room became a trudging ordeal. My feet moved like they were chained together. I fought to keep my eyelids up. I felt like I was in some kind of in-between state. I guess it's what sleepwalkers feel like when they're out and about while they think they're sleeping.

Despite the all-consuming exhaustion, I forced myself to remove my clothes from the dryer, fold them haphazardly, then pack them into my bag.

My eyelids fluttered closed on the walk back to my room. They snapped open when I stepped off the walk into the grass. The jolt shot me awake. What was wrong? I had never felt this way before. My clothes felt like they were sewn with leaden thread. My arms ached by the time I reached the stoop to my dorm.

As I approached the door, Missy and Rhonda exited.

"Hey, we're going to Charlie's, want to come?"

"Can't, I'm beat."

I wanted to go, thought the break might do me some good, but in the end, I declined. Speaking took all my strength. All evening I waited for Duffy. What could he be doing? Now all I wanted was to sleep.

In the reflection on the glass door beneath the halogen light, I took in my visage. Dark baggy flesh rimmed sunken eyes. My ashen lips had begun to crack. I looked like some kind of zombie. My breath gave off a foul emanation that caused Missy and Rhonda to exchange an unmistakable flash of disdain.

"You okay?" Missy asked in response to my lethargy. "You don't look good at all. Maybe you need to get yourself some mint oil."

"Mint oil?"

"My Grandma Nizzie used to give me mint oil when I was sick."

"Fuck your Grandma Nizzie. God, I'm sorry. I'm okay, just dead tired. Must not be eating right."

"Don't study too hard. College is supposed to be fun, remember," Rhonda said. Both beat feet to get away from me, and I couldn't blame them.

Why on earth did I say that? But I was glad they were gone.

Ten-thirty. The time I normally caught my second wind and forged on another two hours. I never retired before midnight. The thought of crawling into bed now riddled me with guilt. Yet, so completely exhausted was I, that I tossed my clothes bag onto Ali's bed and flopped into my own.

Sleep swarmed over me like a hive of angry bees.

****

In sleep, my mind's eye awakened. I saw myself strolling down a sun-drenched country road. But I wasn't alone. A twentyish man my same height walked beside me. I could just make him out in the periphery of my vision.

My dream surfaced in vivid day colors the moment sleep had taken me. My inner sight captured every detail as if I were living the dream in a waking state. It was like I was watching myself on a screen. Yet somehow I could feel my hand in his.

I heard the gravel crackle beneath our feet as we walked. Flanking the rutted way on either side, oceans of white trillium carpeted a lush unbound grassy meadow. Overhead a brilliant sun warmed my flesh. I couldn't have fantasized a more pleasant dream if I tried.

I turned to my companion; I thought at first it was Duffy. But it was someone else. A strange, yet handsome, face that offered a soothing, reassuring smile. A face I had no memory of seeing before. He matched my walk stride for stride.

I smiled out of politeness, for I had no idea why we were together in this engaging place.

His dancing eyes drank in my curves and my beauty. The way he looked at me made me feel special. I could see myself wearing a flowery summer dress dashed with rainbow colors and delicate blue piping for straps. An accenting blue belt drew the eyes immediately to my figure. A shape this man beside me admired carefully.

At first he said nothing, only smiled when I looked his way. Then, as we continued, I spoke. Though I could see his lips form words in response, no sounds entered my head.

His shoulder-length black hair luffed with the gentle breeze. When he turned, I noticed the black and white pattern of his cleric's collar.

Again I observed his lips moving, yet nothing entered my ears. Frustration set in as I strained to hear.

As we rounded a bend in an unhurried pace, an elderly snowy-haired man approached, hunched over from some cruel spinal deformity. He hobbled more than walked, assisted by a walking stick worn smooth through use.

I waited while my companion spoke to the old man in what I assumed was a kindly way. For the old man looked over to me and smiled. I brushed my hair back from my face and returned his smile.

As before, I watched their lips move, knew they were speaking, yet could hear nothing. Though deaf, I believed their exchange pleasant, for the old man's eyes remained fixed on me.

A moment later the old man was gone. I can't say that I know what happened to him.

My companion and I ambled off the beaten path and dove into the sweetly scented landscape.

"*Let me show you Heaven,*" he said.

At last, I heard his voice.

"*Heaven really exists?*" I asked, excited.

I watched myself glide through the flowers though my legs remained stationary; we merely floated along. I felt a rush of exhilaration.

Heaven was just ahead. I was about to witness something other people only spoke of in some religious reverence.

In seconds the road fell far behind.

"*Hurry, go faster,*" he commanded as he moved a full stride ahead and then another.

"*I'm hurrying,*" I called.

My legs worked like pistons to keep up. I feared he would leave me behind. I wanted desperately to see Heaven, to know such a place was real.

The ground beneath our feet rose toward a sprawling piney crest standing staunchly ahead. Heaven was up there?

"*Hurry now,*" he commanded.

There was panic is my breathing; I didn't want to be left behind.

Nearing the crest, a crashing wave of dread shuddered through me. Fear flooded in. The apex of the hill fell under the gloom of shadows. I wanted to slow, but my companion's hand seized mine. At first his touch was gentle, warming. A moment later it turned scabrous.

I felt his hands pull me into the trees. The leafy canopy eradicated the sun. Dark shadows consumed us.

"*Are you a Christian?*" the voice asked.

I offered no response. His rasp of a laugh sent shivers into the core of my spine.

The ground turned barren. The flowers vanished. A fetid stench saturated the air like a heavy rain.

I felt ice rushing through my veins. Why had he taken my hand? It felt all wrong. I tried to look at him; I knew my head was turned in his direction, yet he remained safely out of my vision. How can that be? Fear crawled under my skin the way a cockroach scurries beneath a carpet.

"*Who are you?*" I demanded in a faltering voice. Terror filled my head.

No reply came.

A gnarled hand clamped around mine.

I jerked it, trying to pull free.

"*Are you a priest?*" I persisted, craning my neck to glimpse the form beside me. It was all I could hope for. Yet he remained elusively beyond reach.

"*I am your angel,*" a sepulchral voice said at last.

I yanked my arm. Long bony fingers held it fast.

The demon issued an impassioned earth-rumbling groan. Disfigured claws ripped the front of my dress, peeling back the material to expose my breasts.

A vile, knotted face with jaggedly browned teeth inched close to mine. A pair of stunted goat horns, worn down at the tips, protruded from the creature's spiny-haired forehead.

I forced a scream, felt the air in my chest, but nothing issued forth.

The creature turned to face me squarely, backing me against the knotty bole of an ancient sycamore.

"You whoring bitch, I am your lover."

Scaly hands fondled my breasts, squeezing my nipples cruelly with lust, while a snaking tongue flicked against my smooth silky skin. The creature's hands kneaded my flesh in wanton abandon. Groans of pent-up desire escaped his cracked lips and marched into my head.

I fought. Something held me fast.

"It's been a long time since I've fucked one as nice as you," the satyr said with green-slitted scarlet eyes gazing into mine. My heart pounded with such voracity that I thought it was about to burst. The terror he uncovered deep in my soul only excited him more. A stench that hovered in the air emanated from the creature's mouth every time he opened it in a lustful groan.

Again and again the tongue snaked out from behind the teeth, leaving trails of oozing slime wherever it touched.

In my struggle to break free, I snapped my head to the side. The old man from the road held one of my arms. His lecherous smile beamed while his eyes feasted on my nakedness.

A demon hand abandoned my breast to discard what remained of my dress. The cloth fell away like tissue. Then crudely, as if he were unwrapping a present, he removed the last of my garments.

His laugh became hideous.

I cringed.

The sounds further excited the old man, who began licking his face with a swollen bovine tongue.

"Time to take this bitch to Heaven," the demon laughed.

The satyr pressed against me. I felt his monstrous thing moving on its own like a serpent, seeking the safety of a nest. Prickly hairs jabbed my thighs. A cloven hoof kicked my leg out to open me wider and allow him to penetrate me. No matter how hard I tried to force my legs back together, his furry thighs forced them apart.

"Please let me go," I cried.

"No bitch!" The demon responded by thrusting himself against my mound.

"Have you ever had a beast before?" it asked as casually as if we were talking over coffee. *"Join our little orgy. Matt is with us now."*

The demon's tongue licked out at my breast, rising slowly to my cheek. Fiery red bulging eyes positioned themselves before mine. He delved all the way into my soul. Pulsing veins rose beneath pellucid skin. A strident laugh poured into my head causing me to shudder.

Then one of his clawed fingers probed my private place.

"Hurry up," the old man scowled, *"I want her, too."*

"Shut up, old man. She's yours when I'm finished."

I felt his drilling hardness pressing against me. I wanted to scream, tried to scream, yet nothing issued from my lips. This hideous vision now controlling my sleeping mind terrified me. There was no escape. My heart convulsed on the verge of rupture.

The satyr only laughed at my efforts.

"Struggle no further, bitch, I will free you when I'm ready."

The old man, restless and angered by the demon's dawdling, released one of his hands from mine. I felt a sudden freedom, though only in the slightest way. His eyes moved down while he worked the zipper on his stained trousers.

I seized the opportunity. Jerking my hand free of the old man's now feeble one-handed grip, I twisted free of the demon. I clubbed the hideous face with frantic fists.

His scream ripped the air.

I squirmed free, enduring the caustic bite of animal claws digging into my breast.

Just then I bolted upright, fleeing the dream in that instant. I found myself wrapped tightly in my blanket and sprawled out on the tile floor. My heart hammered against my chest; I fought for air. My head spun. Sweat soaked every inch of my body.

Tortured moments passed away into calm.

A cool, quiescent night surrounded me.

Through a tunnel of darkness I stared at the clock. Four-thirty. I wiped tears from my face. It had all been a terrible dream.

Had I screamed? I must not have, since no one came rushing to my door. But in my dream I screamed the moment I had broken free of the two creatures.

Overcoming the terror still burning as embers in my mind, I sought to recapture the creature's image. Only nebulous impressions drifted back and forth. Something had frightened me out of my slumber. Yet now in the darkness, in the still, even though I trained my mind on it, the very images that haunted me in sleep now eluded me.

Seconds ticked into minutes. Minutes ticked into hours. I lay awake in my bed, staring into the void surrounding me. It was all Missy's fault, with all that crap in the courtyard this afternoon.

Something inside called me to return. Fear kept me vigilant.

In the predawn light, I slipped into a bath robe and headed for the showers. I was alone and relished the opportunity to shower free of the usual morning chaos.

The water was deliciously hot. Steam curled over the curtain seeping throughout the room. I stepped into my own private steamatorium. Normally, in and out traffic prevented this, but today I had it all to herself.

I stood stone-still while streams of warm water rolled down my skin. Moments passed. I reveled in the sensations of fingers dancing across my flesh.

Lathering soap across my body, I stopped, staring down in horror. I threw back the curtain and raced to the mirror. Mist clouded my view. I cleared a portal to my reflection.

Three rubescent claw marks scarred my right breast just above the areola. Blood seeped from the wounds, coalescing with the dripping water. The Bloodstone hung between my breasts.

My scream shook the room, waking the entire wing.

18

Missing Parts

I traipsed across freshly manicured grass with my pack slung over my shoulder. The imminent Algebra quiz staggered my mind. Even after two hours of solitary confinement in a desolate corner of the library, I still realized that it was all hopeless. Every time I attempted those blasted word problems, I invariably arrived at a wrong answer. I hate Algebra and all people who like mathematics. They should be imprisoned on an island somewhere and never allowed to coexist with normal people.

Did you think you were making out a shopping list? My sexist pig professor would ask.

As I approached Camp Pendleton, Missy sat on the concrete stoop outside the dorm with her legs outstretched, luxuriating in a bronzing afternoon sun. Her eyes locked on mine in a strange way as I approached.

"You're taking it rather well, considering," she said.

"Taking what well?"

"You haven't heard?"

"Heard what?"

"It's been going around campus all afternoon. The police fished a body out of the creek."

"What? Oh my God!"

I began to quake. My books toppled out of my hands. Strength slipped away from me like water down a drain. My skin turned to parchment.

Missy leapt up just in time to support me before I fell. She really wasn't so bad.

"Sorry, I thought you knew. I heard an hour ago at Reynolds. The state police found the body in a creek about sixty miles from here."

"Oh my God, no," I cried.

"Come on, let's get you inside. You don't look too good."

Duffy arrived out of breath and sweating. Missy and I were in my room, joined by Rhonda. We stared at the television tuned to the local station. A meaningless hemorrhoid commercial occupied the screen.

"You heard," he said softly, slipping a comforting arm around me.

"A few minutes ago. Is it..."

"We're waiting to see what they say," Rhonda said, keeping her eyes fixed on the screen.

"We just have to wait. No one I talked to could confirm it," Missy added.

Duffy held me but said nothing. My trembling continued despite Duffy's efforts to soothe me.

"Police today removed a body from the shallow creek running through the Beau Bien Forest Preserve," the anchor said devoid of emotion.

"Male or female?" Rhonda pressed anxiously.

I began to mewl.

Missy notched up the volume.

"Then only one body was found?" Duffy asked.

No answer came.

"Trish, we don't know anything," Duffy offered. He could see the fear rising inside me.

"This was the scene shortly after eleven this morning with the county coroner and state police. Two hikers spotted the body approximately two hours before this footage was taken."

Quenby knocked on my open door, standing with only his head peeking into the room.

"Come in, Quenby, you've heard, too."

All eyes stared in horror as two attendants transferred a limp rubber bag from the creek bed to the back of a waiting black station wagon.

"Oh God, there's..." I stopped myself. I watched Nick Logan working the water's edge. The FBI agent I spoke with in Cleveland crossed the screen moments later.

"Oh my God, it's Ali," I said, dropping down onto my bed. I knew it without a doubt.

"I was worried, Trish, so I hurried right over. I hope I'm not intruding," Quenby offered.

Missy, who had been sitting at my desk, wiped away the sudden rush of tears rolling out of her eyes.

"We have been informed that the body is that of an eighteen to twenty-two year-old male and efforts are currently underway to make a positive identification."

"Sweet Jesus," Missy moaned in relief, fanning herself with her hand.

"It's Matt. Ali's dead, too," I cried, burying my head into Duffy's shoulder.

"Listen to me. We don't know that. We don't know the identity of the body yet. And we have nothing linking Matt's disappearance to Ali's. The news said only one body was found," Duffy said.

"What about Matt's fiance?"

****

I trudged down the stairs of the cultural studies building with my head hung low and my mind mired in I don't know what. I seemed incapable of pulling myself out of a black depression that rose up like prison walls around me. Even acing a conjugation quiz in Russian failed to elevate my spirit out of its depths. I just wanted the day to be over when a big hulk knocked into me as I reached the last stair. My books toppled like water cascading over the falls, and when I looked up Nick Logan stared into my eyes.

"Excuse me," he said with a gruffness that would have intimidated anyone who didn't know who he was; his eyes were obscured by a baseball cap pulled down to cover his forehead. I noticed the coaching staff shirt he wore and the clipboard he carried. For a long moment I stood there dumbfounded while he retrieved my books and stacked them back into my hand.

"3-0-9," he whispered. Then he took the stairs two at a time and disappeared into the darkness of the building.

I continued down the last stair and headed to my left, opposite of the way I had intended to go. I strolled the uncluttered walkways to re-enter the building using the north side doors. Once inside I climbed to the first landing and paused for at least a minute, watching the doors below me. No one entered in my wake. No one had even paused at the doors to peer inside. I felt comfortable no one had taken an interest in our brief exchange.

The idea of a clandestine meeting with a government agent quickened my heart beat and pommelled the depression that kept crowding into my head. Did he have information? Could he have learned something about Ali's disappearance?

Reaching the third floor, I chanced to glance over my shoulder one more time to reassure my nagging mind that all was safe so far, then I walked quickly to the designated room and tried the door. Locked? I took furtive scans up and down the floor and saw no one in a baseball cap.

Now what? I tried to think like an undercover agent. God knows I've seen enough movies. I should know what to do. But I stood there waiting at the door. After a few minutes the corridor cleared as the last of the students made their way into classrooms and study labs.

No sooner did I leave the designated rendez-vous when Nick emerged from another room and motioned me inside.

He closed the door on an unused language lab and pointed to one of the desks with walls around it. He took the next one over.

"I saw you on the tube," I said.

"I figured you would. I need your help, Patricia."

"I need *your* help! Somebody's trying real hard to keep me from finding out what happened to Ali. Every time I ask questions I have to look over my shoulder. Matt's death is not a coincidence."

"Could Ali have become involved with any of the drug dealers on campus?"

"Damnit, I told you Ali stayed clear of drugs. If you're looking to bust everyone who's used drugs on campus, then I'm wasting my time."

I rose in anger and pushed the chair back. Nick's hand clamped on my forearm. When I looked over at him I saw something in his eyes.

"You're not FBI. Who the hell are you? It's time you started giving me something!"

I waited. Nick read my eyes. He must have had to decide in that moment whether to open up to me or walk out. He glanced quickly at his watch, weighed his options.

"I'm DEA. I head a task force."

"What kind of task force? To bust college kids doing drugs? And how does Ali fit into this?"

"We're tracking a criminal ring that kidnaps young women and sells them to the Colombian druglords."

I fell back down into my chair. My stomach sank until it felt like I was going to retch.

"When the druglords tire of the women they buy they dispose of them. I need your help. Patricia, I have enough evidence to shut down the campus police force and a couple dozen small time dealers here. That's not what I'm after. If Ali's been snatched, her life is at stake here. I've already lost three young women and two of my toughest agents in Colombia. We have to find the scum that orchestrating this in the U.S."

I stumbled for words during the span of Nick's pause. It was all rushing into my head. I glimpsed a vision of Ali's bloodied body slumped on a bare wood floor.

"If the slave traders took Ali, they'll need a way to get her to the coast for transport to Colombia. We've intercepted what we believe is their courier and hope they haven't been able to move her yet. That's means we've still got a chance. But I can't work the inside of the campus. And if whoever took her smells us, he'll dump his trade and disappear. I'm trying as hard as I can, but I need your help."

"When you say dump his trade, you mean he'll let her go?"

"He'll kill her to protect his identity. The only way we can save her is to get to him."

"What can I do?" I shifted in my chair to get closer to Nick and listened, using all my powers of concentration. When he remained silent I decided to press for information.

"How long has Matt been dead?"

"Couldn't tell. Water did a job on the body. Why?"

"Merrifield said he spoke to Matt at home. How could he have if Matt never made it home?"

"I think the Matt Evans link's a dead end."

"Why?"

"Matt Evans was a cult killing."

"How can you know that?"

"They have a very distinctive way of saying it. They removed his little fingers and genitals and stuffed them into his rectum."

I cringed at the visions the words conjured.

"Then they ended his suffering."

For a long moment I couldn't think. I needed deep breathes to keep my stomach from convulsing into my throat. The torture Matt must have gone through before…

"I'm sorry. I had to be graphic. I can't think of any other way to convince you of my concern."

"Wait, if Ali had unknowingly become involved with the same cult, could that tie her and Matt to your investigation?"

"Not likely. We would have found their bodies together if she had been involved. Our suspect moves from campus to campus. We picked up his trail at the University of Oregon in Eugene, then later at the University of California at Santa Barbara. From what you've given us earlier about Ali Goodfellow, there's a good chance she became his next victim."

"What does he look like?"

"We don't know. He plants false identities in the school's computers. We have experts right now working Ranhurst's enrollment hoping to find a link back to California."

"But you're saying you think Ali's still alive?"

"If it's our man who took her, yes. He won't get a dime for damaged goods. He'll take good care of her until he makes his delivery. Then only God can help her."

"It is feasible then that Ali might still be on campus?"

Nick checked his watch nervously while I spoke.

"A very remote possibility. But highly unlikely. He would have stashed her in a safe place until he could arrange for a courier to pick her up. We've been intercepting every known Colombian courier moving into or near this state. Patricia, we're doing everything we can to keep them from making a move to transport her. If she's the one."

"And if she's not?"

"Then...I don't know."

"Did you learn anything from Matt's death that might help link him to Ali's disappearance?"

"Our time's up. This place is going to get busy in about three minutes. You leave first. I'll be in touch."

I rose and turned for the door. Nick took my arm.

"I just came from a missing girl's parents in Texas. I've been through the girl's things a hundred times, but I still go back, hoping to find something to link our victims to the bastard who's doing this. They told me they hold an annual candlelight vigil at their church on the eve of the Feast of Michaelmas. The day their daughter disappeared. That was four years ago. They're still praying for her safe return. I don't have the heart to tell them she's never coming home."

"How can you be sure?"

"Because that's how these scum operate. We're doing everything we can. I don't want to lose this one any more than you. Patricia, don't give up on her. Right now you're doing more than anyone else can to force our man to the surface. And remember, we're behind you on this."

I said nothing. I knew Nick could see the fear in my eyes. His words not only quelled those fears but zapped the depression that had kept me ineffective in the past few days. He had breathed new life into me. I left with a renewed resolve to continue on. Someone somewhere could help me, and I had to persevere until I uncovered that person.

****

I hesitated, standing before Room 212 in the Shreveport Residence Hall. One day had passed since the news of the body being found in the creek was broadcast. Elaine's telephone call had been abrupt and cryptic, and it came less than three hours after the news announced the body in the creek was Matt Evans.

Elaine appeared promptly following my knock. Her face was lifeless and sullen, her eyes a portrait of anguish and fear.

"I'm Trish Van Worten."

"Sure. Why don't we walk." Elaine's voice was filled with a false bravado that failed to mask her anxiety. Her eyes revealed more than a concern over Matt's death. I read something deeper, something sinister in the way her eyes searched mine.

I felt my heart banging like a bass drum. This was going to be a difficult exchange; I knew it from the way Elaine's eyes darted. I had no idea of just how awkward it might become. What did Elaine know? Whatever it is, it must be important for her to initiate this meeting between us.

Elaine remained silent and tentative until we were well beyond the building and isolated from other passing students.

I knew my silence was mandatory. Now was a time for patience. Let Elaine open up. Ask only what was absolutely necessary.

"You want to know about that guy I dated from Delta Rho," Elaine started, as if she had called upon some deeply buried inner strength to produce those first words. Her voice lacked force; her cadence was broken. Elaine, herself, was lost as to how to begin.

"I don't know what happened to my roommate. But I believe it's somehow linked to that frat house. It's no coincidence that she dated Matt Evans from Delta Rho last year, and now he's dead and she's missing."

I realized my interruption had further eroded Elaine's fragile confidence. The awkward pause could mean Elaine had changed her mind. Whatever was locked away in her head was maybe destined to remain there.

"If this is too difficult for you, it's okay. I understand. But could you tell me if there is any reason I should *not* suspect Delta Rho?"

"I knew Ali Goodfellow. I saw her at the frat house with Matt a few times. She's really beautiful. I can see why Matt pursued her so. But I don't remember it too clearly." Elaine paused.

I watched the inner maelstrom churning behind Elaine's eyes.

"Trish, what I'm going to tell you, I've never revealed to another living soul...I can't even face it myself. Promise me you will tell no one what you're going to hear."

"Promise."

I prepared myself. *What had happened at Delta Rho?*

Elaine stopped with a jolt. A passing couple seized her tongue. She waited, her lips thin across her face, until they passed out of range.

"I'm only telling you this because...maybe it will help you. I dated Reid for about two months...in early spring. At first everything was great. No pressure; he just wanted to be with me. We had fun together, and I was really falling for him. Don't get me wrong. I'm usually pretty sus-picious with guys. I don't fall for the first guy who buys me expensive gifts. He wanted me to go to bed with him, but I told him I wasn't ready."

I stared forward, cataloging commonalties between Ali and Elaine: both were stunning and shapely. Their looks were sure to attract hungry male stares.

I glanced at the path that led to the Agricul-ture building. I worried that if I even looked at Elaine, if my eyes caught hers at the wrong mo-ment, the Ranhurst junior might lose her nerve. Then I would end up with nothing.

My heart pounded in anticipation. I rubbed the sweat from my palms as we walked.

"After a while we started getting closer. We did more, but we always stopped short of doing *it*. One weekend, he literally begged me on his knees to make love, and after breaking down my resistance, I gave in; I said I loved him and he said he loved me."

Elaine's voice bowed under the weight of the terrible secret pushing its way to the surface.

I guided Elaine onto a deserted pathway. Spotting an empty bench isolated within a grove of maples, I hoped to remain segregated from others on the walkway. From Elaine's faltering demeanor, I sensed she must be reaching the crux of her story.

"Reid said his uncle had a cabin by Arrowhead Lake, north of here." Elaine stopped, her eyes welling with tears. It took a moment for her to choke down the pain.

"He said we'd go there for the night. He could use the cabin whenever it was vacant."

I parted my lips to speak, held my words in check, sensing Elaine needed to continue while she had control.

"We went to the cabin. It turned into a real bizarre experience. We drank...but not alot. Then we laid together on a luxurious rug in front of the fireplace. I remember it rained that night, so Reid started a fire. As the evening progressed, we undressed."

Elaine took my forearm. I motioned toward the trees off to our right.

"I'm not a slut."

"You want to sit down? We shouldn't be interrupted."

I pointed to a stone bench in the deserted hollow. The wind purled through the leaves. The seclusion helped Elaine. I knew I had to keep Elaine talking until it all came out. For both our sakes.

"Before we could make love, I think I passed out. It was really strange because I dreamed I was on a bed with Reid and he was doing all kinds of things to me."

"What kinds of things?" I asked behind a clinical visage.

"Sexual things, I mean I was doing things to him, too. Things that I would never do. Something had come over me. I wanted sex so bad I couldn't stop myself. The more he did, the more I liked it, and the more I wanted. I became an insatiable nymphomaniac."

"Had you ever experienced that before?"

"Never. And I've never experienced it since."

Elaine hesitated.

My mind raced back through space and time. Something was trying to buoy to the surface. But what? I was back in Matt's room in the closet. What did that girl say...? What was she begging for...? Nothing at first came to me, then I remembered. She was asking, no begging, for love candy. Was that a drug these creeps were using on Elaine and that girl? I had no time to wonder.

"It got worse."

Elaine broke down finally, letting tears flow to vent the trapped pressure. A moment later she recovered.

"Then another guy joined us in bed. Reid kept moving me around, telling me to do things with this other guy."

"Elaine," I interrupted, risking that nothing would silence the girl now. "Why do you say it was like a dream?"

"The light was so bright, I could barely see. And it didn't feel real. Except for the excitement I was experiencing. I've never had anything like that before. I wanted more; I didn't want the sex to stop."

"Did you recognize the other man with you?"

"No, he wore a bird's mask. Some kind of hawk or eagle or something like that. It had feathers. I wasn't sure what it was."

Elaine left the bench and moved behind me. I stared forward.

"I had never experienced that kind of sexual gratification before in my life. But at the same time, it frightened me—I was out of control. I couldn't stop it. Reid wanted more and I gave it to him."

I choked down my own tears listening to Elaine's faint cries behind me.

"Elaine, it's okay. You can stop if this is too difficult for you."

"I'm okay. I need to get it all out. I need you to know what happened. The next morning I awoke on the living room floor under a blanket. Reid was asleep beside me. He said I'd gotten drunk and passed out. I never told him about my dream. He swears we never made love that night. But I know different."

"Elaine, did you do drugs that night?"

"I don't do drugs. Alcohol's my limit."

"Could Reid have spiked your drink?"

"Maybe...I don't know. After that weekend Reid was...I don't know, not really cold, but he seemed less interested in me. He no longer wanted to make love. He never dumped me outright, he just called less and less until I finally realized it was over."

I rose. Engulfed in my own thoughts, I started back for the walkway.

Elaine came up beside me; her eyes were glassed over with tears.

I looked deep beyond those mirrors of agony, searching hers. What was going on at Delta Rho house? What kind of perverts were these creeps?

"I don't know if it helps you."

"It could help a lot. If Matt took Ali to the cabin, it could give me a solid direction. Do you think you can find that cabin again? Can you take me there?"

"I don't have a car. But yeah, I think I could. There was this large carved owl sitting on a tree stump on the walk to the cabin door. I remember it because it was so intricately carved, it looked almost real."

"When can we go?"

"Saturday. But why? You think maybe Matt and Ali went there?"

"I don't know. But maybe...just maybe, Ali went there after returning to Ranhurst."

"Oh, one more thing. After I returned from the cabin I was very sick for two days. I just figured I'd caught a bug or something. By Tuesday I was back to normal."

"Did Reid return this year?"

"Graduated. I never had anything to do with anyone from Delta Rho after that."

19

A Falling Out

I slumped in a retral chair in a stuffy lecture hall. Two dozen rows down, Professor Slater delivered his drone dissertation as if he had ejected those same words a thousand times before. The words were faint echoes in my untuned ears.

Like many around me, I doodled on my notebook, my mind drifting from one subject to another with little concentration being applied to Astronomy. I thought about what Elaine had revealed to me and how much pain it must have caused her to open something like that up. Tomorrow we would go to the cabin. Duffy had arranged to use his roommate's car. I could only hope there would be something there that might help me figure out what happened to Ali.

Someone across the hall asked a question.

I politely lifted my head to catch a poor rendering of a planetary orbit on the chalkboard. A moment later my mind drifted to Duffy. What was he doing at this moment? Was he thinking about me? Did my image stick in his mind the way his stuck in mine?

I glanced at the clock. Another twenty-two minutes. A jabbing pain of guilt shot through me. I really should be attentive; I needed this course. But...

"On the night of the twenty-eighth..." Slater continued.

Suddenly, I pulled myself straight in my chair. The twenty-eighth? An alarm went off inside my head. Why had that struck a cord in my brain?

I strained with renewed and ardent interest to recapture the lecture. I had missed the opening statements leading to the twenty-eighth. Now I was lost.

I waved in a frenzy.

"Yes?" Slater asked, gazing over the rim of his black-framed glasses. He showed a visible disdain for interruptions.

"What happens on the twenty-eighth?"

"Oh look, she's not dead after all. Who wants to know?" Slater spewed in a feeble attempt at humor.

A few smiled. One or two chuckled.

"Patricia Van Worten. What happens on the twenty-eighth?"

"Well, Miss Van Worten, thank God I've found at least something that interests you."

Peals of laughter broke out.

I sunk deeper into my chair.

"What I said was, the full moon rises on the night of the twenty-eighth. So Miss Van Worten, are we in a waxing or waning cycle right now?"

Oh great, ask a question, get a question. I hate professors who do that.

Waxing...waning...waxing...waning. *Take a guess.*

"Waxing?" Wild guess.

"Very good. On the twenty-eighth the lunar cycle reaches its fulgent climax. You know, werewolves and that sort of thing. They say the full moon affects people in weird ways. Anyway, I hope I've satisfied your curiosity. Oh, and this full moon will be extra special. We will also experience a lunar eclipse between the hours of 9 P.M. and 1 A.M. Perhaps Miss Van Worten, you'll go back to sleep now so I can go on with my lecture?"

"Sure, don't let me hold you up any longer," I injected in a weak shot at humor. No one laughed.

I wanted to crawl beneath my chair. Instead, I stared at my notebook.

The entire class had turned to stare at me. God, I felt like a cretin.

Why was the twenty-eighth so important? I ransacked my memory, tossing out irrelevant bits of information. A full moon on the twenty-eighth; why did that keep playing on my mind? Matt Evans.

"Matt Evans and the twenty-eighth," I whispered as the class filed out the lecture hall doors.

Matt had lined through the twenty-eighth on his calendar in red. The day must have been important to Matt, though it seemingly bore no relevance to the full moon on that night.

I was the last to exit the hall. But before leaving, I stared at the chalkboard, hoping for inspiration. The twenty-eighth bobbed to the surface of my mind. It meant something.

20

Anyone Speak Latin?

Quenby, Duffy and I stared at a rectangular screen about the size of a 13-inch television. However, this instrument had three rows of calibration dials along the side and magnified things to a thousand times their normal size.

Quenby adjusted a dial that brought the Bloodstone into sharp focus under a five hundred times magnification. This was Quenby's first opportunity to really study the stone. With a researcher's precision, he began cataloging each detail looming on the screen.

The elephantine size forced the Bloodstone to surrender every nuance of its mystery to us.... Almost.

The spiraling specks of red stood out in stark contrast to the murky background. But what captured all our attention was the three specks of glinting crystalline embedded beneath the surface. They glistened like diamonds submerged beneath a cloudy substrate.

"This is most remarkable," Quenby commented. The stone's mesmerizing colors held his eyes fast.

"Fine, but what about the glypo..." I blurted, worried that at any moment someone might enter the lab.

"Glyptograph," Quenby interjected.

"What is a glyptograph?" Duffy asked leaning in around us in curious fashion. His initial indifference had suddenly turned to rapt fascination.

Quenby handed Duffy the FAX.

"Who's Emory?"

"My uncle back in London. He asked me to check for a glyptograph. That would authenticate the stone as one of the original Bloodstones."

"It also says here the Bloodstone dates back centuries."

"Look at the setting. You see how these fine strands contour to the stone's shape."

"This is no ordinary stone, is it Quenby?" I asked, my voice falling away into the silent void between us. When Quenby turned his face away from the machine to look at me, I saw something strange in his eyes. A concern really. This had to have something to do with Ali's disappearance.

But how? How could some odd stone be involved?

"I don't believe so."

Quenby gently eased the stone to its flat side, searching for our purpose in the lab.

"There it is," he said, amazed, yet at the same time, unaffected by what he found. Almost as if he expected to find it. He eased away, allowing Duffy and me a look.

"Je-sus..." I said in a whisper.

We peered at the screen with a childlike fascination. I held my breath so as not to fog up the glass.

"I don't believe this," Duffy uttered.

"They're..."

Quenby moved in closer and repositioned the stone for maximum magnification.

"Good work, Holmes," I said, setting my hand on his shoulder. He looked up to me, offered a faint smile. He obviously agreed with my choice of nicknames for him.

"Thank you." He said it as if it had been the first time someone had complimented him.

Duffy edged in for a better look.

"Those markings...are words, aren't they?" I asked.

"Latin, Medieval Latin, I think..."

Quenby studied the curvature of each line engraved into the stone. Only the most delicate hand could have possibly formed such etchings. To the naked eye, the glyptograph appeared as an impurity on the stone's face. But under intense magnification, the stone offered up markings that became words. So precise and so exact were they, that each had the breadth and depth of a mosquito's hair.

"How could they have been made?" I asked.

No one had an answer.

Quenby, I sensed, had suspicions. But he swallowed them.

"Even more remarkable, these stones go back at least eight centuries. Bloodstones originated in Medieval times as amulets against evil. Martyr's stones they were called back then. If you believe that sort of thing."

We all leaned in until our heads touched. Duffy lifted his to look at me. I was so absorbed by the stone's mystery, I never looked up. His smile went unnoticed.

"Can you decipher them?" Duffy said.

"Pencil and paper," Quenby said.

I offered up a pen; Duffy pulled paper from his book.

Quenby bounced back and forth between paper and stone. With an artist's hand, he duplicated the markings as best as he could. When he finished, he stepped back from the screen to study the paper. A moment later, perplexed, he gazed at the gem again to compare his markings to those on the stone.

"...*meum animus...esse...tuus.*"

Quenby then adjusted a few more dials and shifted the plate on which the stone rested. His alterations repositioned the stone ever so slightly onto another side.

"I'll need a more powerful lens in order to be absolutely certain of one of these words. It starts with *ASMO*...that's all I can get. The words are definitely Medieval Latin, the language used by the church up until the thirteenth century."

"What do the words mean?" I asked.

Quenby said nothing. Instead, he studied the stone under the scrutiny of the powerful lens. Something he saw, or rather something he felt deep inside, kept him silent.

"I'm sorry," he said at last.

"What do the words mean?"

"Something, something...thine," Quenby muttered, staring for a long time at the words.

"No wait, be thine. Something, something, be thine."

"Quenby?"

Quenby's eyes rose off the paper to mine.

"What does this *really* mean?" I asked.

"Very little, I suspect. If you want my honest opinion, this is probably an imitation of an old religious amulet. Most likely created in this century."

"Come on, Quenby, we're not that stupid. We've seen the markings. You don't just sit down with an Exacto knife and cut Latin words into a stone," Duffy said.

"Okay, think of it like a counterfeiter. A fat-bellied old geezer sits with his eyes peering through a magnifying glass to carefully scribe these markings in a stone. How do you think a counterfeiter makes a fake plate?"

"We know *why* a counterfeiter does it, now why would someone engrave a stone like this?"

"Europeans are superstitious. During the last few centuries people in Europe actually wore periapts, religious charms as you Yanks might know them, to protect them from evil. Either of you remember your history of the Salem witch hunts and things like that?"

"Yeah, so what are you saying?"

"Simply that you may have stumbled upon an old amulet used to protect the wearer from evil conjurings. I could go into fascinating detail concerning the fears and superstitions of the type of people who believed in these things. But we know better. Witches and demons just don't exist. And anyway, the only protective value of a stone comes from its use as a projectile."

We all tried to laugh, but none of us could find the humor.

Maybe it was the way Quenby spoke, or the inflection in his explanation, but I was certain crucial parts of his story were conveniently omitted. Another thing missing was Quenby's own conviction. Maybe that lack of conviction grew out of his inability to discern one of the glyptograph words.

Sounds in the hall filtered through the door. I snatched the stone out of the instrument and slid it into my pocket.

Students filed into the lab, glancing with little interest at the three of us huddled across the room.

"I'd like a better look under a more powerful glass, if you wouldn't mind?" Quenby said, tucking the paper with the Latin words into his book.

I looked to Duffy.

Duffy's eyes flashed caution. They also sent uncertainty about what the British student had said.

"Sure. Can you get us to a better lens?" I asked.

"Perhaps you'll leave the stone with me, and I'll return it after I've had a better look."

"How about you tell me when and where, and I bring the stone. I think somebody at Ranhurst wants this thing, and I'm not letting go of it until I find out why. This could be our only link to Ali right now."

"I understand. Let me talk to a few people. I think for the time being, though, you should keep it safe. I don't think it has any dollar value as a gem, but it may be valuable to a collector of antiquities."

"Could it have anything to do with Ali's disappearance?"

"I don't see how."

After leaving the lab, Quenby proceeded toward Administration, where he could access a FAX machine to send the words he uncovered to his uncle. If anyone could decipher them, we had to hope his Uncle Emory could.

21

Hooks Are A Clue

Saturday morning. I stood anxiously outside what could only be described as a frog-gut green Ford Escort in the parking lot waiting for Elaine. Somebody had to have been color blind to buy a car like that. Suffice it to say, I was glad it wasn't Duffy's.

Duffy tapped out the beat of the song on the radio against the steering wheel. His eyes lingered on me in my tight cutoff jeans while I paced back and forth. There were certainly better things to do than what I had planned.

I approached Elaine the moment she exited the dorm. There was no mistaking the anxiety swarming over Elaine's face and the betrayal flashing in her eyes.

"I needed him to drive. I don't have a car," I offered.

"You promised..."

"I only told him we're going to check out a place where Ali might have been. Elaine, I promise, I said nothing about what you confided in me. Please believe me. I'd never betray you."

The words helped.

Duffy played chauffeur by asking for the first general direction, then remaining silent.

Three hours and a dozen wrong turns later, we finally arrived in an area where Elaine believed the cabin would be found. That came only after she spotted Arrowhead Lake. I breathed a sigh of relief that her memory had held up so far.

Once on the road skirting the water, we drove at twenty-five miles an hour in one gigantic circle. We slowed often, enduring angry blasts from cars in our wake while we searched.

I detected a mounting concern on Elaine's face. There was no other way to proceed. I knew this would pull up painful memories. I knew bringing her here would force her to relive every second of what she had revealed to me. Inside, I prayed the trip would turn up something.

Could I dare to hope to find Ali alive and imprisoned in the cabin? Nick had said the one who snatched Ali would need a safe place to hold her until he could move her to the coast. I cautioned myself toward restraint; I was working on pure supposition at this point.

At a woody bend, Duffy slowed as he scanned a gravel road meandering into the trees. To his dismay, he realized the only way to find this cabin was going to be to drive down every road. Even then, we faced the very real possibility that so many of the cabins had been identically constructed that they became indistinguishable to Elaine.

After seven consecutive failures, Elaine's confidence crumbled. After all, she was only there once, it was near dark when they arrived, and she never really spent much time looking the place over.

She did remember a cupola on the roof with a painted rooster and a carved owl on the tree stump before the door. The only thing going for us so far was that none of the cabins we approached matched that description.

Duffy eased off the main road again onto a rutted path that snaked up to a boxy cabin overlooking a secluded bight in the lake.

Elaine pointed out the owl on the stump. My heart thumped. A sign of hope. I looked up. The weather vain also matched her description.

"This could be it," she said, releasing for the first time excitement for having brought us to this place.

"How many people you figure paint their roosters," I said.

"So what do we do now?" Duffy asked.

I answered him with a look fraught with devious intent.

"Oh no, I don't think we should go there."

"What, I'm just going to see if anyone's home."

"Yeah, right. Place looks deserted to me."

I ran my fingers over the owl's woody plumage as I passed it. Elaine and Duffy remained in the car. Even before knocking, I craned my neck for a glimpse inside the cabin. No signs of life within.

When no one answered my repeated knocks, I shrugged and walked around the structure, peering in each window as I went.

"I'd better make sure you don't do anything we'll regret," Duffy said as he ran up beside me. There was no hiding the concern in his eyes.

Elaine never moved from the back seat. The sight must have rekindled those memories she had buried.

Duffy reconnoitered the terrain. Though other cabins dotted the area, lush thickets of beech and pine secluded this cabin from its neighbors.

"This is the place," I said, spying the living room through a filmy window. Directly across from where I stood was a large stone fireplace. The layout closely matched Elaine's description.

"We can't be sure, Trish. We need Elaine to say that."

A moment later Elaine appeared around the corner.

"I didn't want to be alone," she said.

"Is this the place?"

Elaine studied the interior.

"I'm sure it is. I remember the furnishings."

"You said you were only in the living room. As far as you know, you never made it to the..."

"Right." Elaine was sharp with her reply.

"So, how do we get in?" I asked.

"Look for a key on the door molding or under a potted plant?"

Our brief search bore no key. To get in, you had to come with the key.

"Can you jimmy a lock?" I asked.

"Who me?" Duffy replied.

While Duffy worked at the rear door, I scanned the surroundings. The dead bolt had been engaged.

"So, now we know where the place is. And we know there's no one inside. Can we go?" Elaine said, backing away to retrace her steps back to the car.

"No. I need to look around inside."

"That's a job for the police. Why don't we just let them handle this."

"We can't, Duffy, trust me on this."

Elaine receded further from us, her courage waning with each second.

"Duffy, we need to get in there. Police need probable cause and a warrant, we don't."

"Right, and we call that Breaking and Entering, boys and girls."

I palmed a rock, and without warning, tossed it through the window pane nearest the dead bolt.

Duffy spun around clumsily, nervously scanning, hoping no one heard the crashing glass.

A second later I stepped over the glass shards on the cabin floor.

"Okay, so now we're in. What next?" Duffy said, his voice caught with a sarcastic edge.

Like it or not, I needed to know if this place had anything to do with Ali. Looking back at the innocence of Duffy's face, I figured him to be one of those nerds who never once in his life got into trouble. This whole encounter probably sent his stomach into convulsions right now. I figured some things are more important than broken glass and a few angry words.

"We're just three college students looking for a place to crash for the night. Got it. We get caught, we just play dumb. So they make us pay for the window, so what."

Elaine stopped at the edge of the living room and stared at the fireplace. Her eyes revealed that it had all just come flooding back to her. The amateurish oil painting of the lake that hung over the mantle erased any doubt lingering in her mind. Stepping forward, she reached for the picture.

"Don't touch that!" Duffy yelled.

"Don't touch anything," I added.

Duffy cast me a worried look, then began searching the room. For what, he had no idea. He used a pencil off the counter to open cabinets in a galley kitchen no larger than necessary to accommodate one person.

Half of this neglected cabin was living space, with a battered sofa, a couple of chairs around a table, and the fireplace.

The galley kitchen adjoined the living area. Beat-up stove in desperate need of a good cleaning, a small refrigerator that vibrated on wobbly feet when it kicked on, and a stainless steel sink marred with everything from wine to coffee to who knows what.

I scanned the living room, hoping to spot something that might give me inspiration. I couldn't let Duffy know I had no idea what to do now that we were inside. But my search turned up nothing out of the ordinary.

Duffy announced the absence of food on the premises and the fact that the trash had been removed from under the sink. Okay, so the last person to leave had enough sense to prevent rodents from rummaging around inside. The cabin was intentionally unoccupied, at least for the present. And from all indications, we expected no one to come driving up while we were there.

The other half of the cabin provided the sleeping space. Two eight-by-fourteen bedrooms, both large enough for a double bed, but leaving little room otherwise. A bathroom between the two bedrooms had a rust-stained shower and a toilet that appeared worse than the kitchen sink. The wash basin was no bigger than two hands and had so many cracks and chips out of it that it could probably no longer hold water.

From an investigative standpoint, this cabin was impeccably clean, except for the broken glass on the floor. No photographs of people who lived there, no mail envelopes or receipts that might offer up some clue as to who had recently occupied the place.

While Duffy searched one bedroom, I entered the other. The design allowed bathroom access from either bedroom. Very accommodating, I thought peering into the small cubicle. The glass in the tiny bathroom window had multiple cracks taped over with cellophane tape.

Duffy's head peered in through the opposite doorway. We looked at each other, shrugging. So why did this nagging feeling persist that there was something here? Every time I went to leave the bedroom, something tugged me back in. By now I had learned to trust my intuition. There had to be something here.

Both bedrooms were unremarkable. A bed, a narrow dresser, a night stand with a lamp. No telephones, no intrusions, complete privacy.

"So the place is clean," Duffy said, leaving his room and joining me.

"I can't find a thing," I finally admitted, frustration brimming in my voice. Yet I had to turn back for another look.

Elaine stopped at the entrance to the bedroom.

"Elaine, does this look like the room?"

"I don't know. I can't be sure. Like I said, the light was so bright, I could hardly see."

I suspected Elaine knew she had been in this room before. Doing a slow three-sixty, I studied every inch of the room. *Bingo!* Without speaking, I hurried to the other bedroom and performed the same careful ritual. Then I returned, unable to conceal the excitement of what I had uncovered.

"What's different about these two rooms?" I posed to Duffy.

He re-observed the other bedroom then rejoined me.

"The hooks," he said, pointing up as if he were answering a professor's trick question in Psychology class.

"Exactly. Why does this bedroom have ceiling hooks while the other room doesn't?"

"Beats me," Duffy said, turning to Elaine.

I stood in the bathroom. I turned another slow circle as if again studying each inch of wall, ceiling and floor. Coming out, I gazed up at the hooks then re-entered the bathroom.

"What are you thinking?" Duffy said, now confused by my growing fascination. My face had turned to stone. My stomach churned as I put the pieces of what I had discovered together.

"Elaine, it might best if you wait in the car."

"No, I'm okay. Maybe I can help. Why?"

I paused. *Should I say what my mind had assembled?* Everything slowly began to fall into place.

"I got a *bad* feeling. Duffy, look at this."

I pointed to the bathroom, then took him out of the bedroom into the small hallway.

"I don't get it," Duffy said.

"Dead space. You don't build a cabin with dead space."

Duffy now realized my intimation. There was space unaccounted for between the bedrooms. Was it?

I opened a closet door between the two bedroom entrances. The closet appeared normal enough. Sheets and pillow cases, blankets and three shelves of towels. Everything you'd expect to find in a vacation cabin.

Then I spotted it.

Along the upper edge, the wall seam had separated. I ran my finger along the seam, then pushed on the back wall. Nothing moved.

I pushed again, this time harder. Still nothing.

"You think it could be?" Duffy asked, squeezing a hand in to push along with me. The wall never budged.

I thought for a long moment. Then I planted my feet in the doorway, placed both hands palms up under a waist-high shelf and lifted. The wall inched up. As it did, it rotated.

The passive rear panel was really a door secured in place with a pin into a hole in the floor. Only when you lifted could it be opened.

As I suspected, nobody built cabins with dead space. The false wall rotated to access a small unlit alcove. A rush of stale air brushed our faces on its way to freedom.

Even before I entered that place, I knew what I would find. I knew because I needed an explanation for why Elaine had the dream, and why she said the light was so blinding. The hooks in the ceiling had a very real, and very perverted, purpose.

I breast-stroked through cobwebs. Inside this unused place, I located a battery operated light mounted at eye level. The fledgling illumination flowed over a dusty metal folding chair and a chest-high shelf. A step ladder leaned against the slats beneath the shelf. Someone used it to reach the narrow shelf a foot from the ceiling.

I coughed out the dust clogging my lungs.

Two compact video cameras sat diabolically perched six feet apart on the high shelf. Each lens was an inch from the wall. Each camera connected to a nine-inch color television monitor.

I flipped a switch for a bank of outlets. Instantly the monitors popped on. That same moment an icy chill swept through the three of us as the bedroom bloomed onto the screens. The bed became the focal point. But even with daylight pouring through the windows, the LOW LIGHT warning flashed on the screens. There was insufficient illumination for videotaping. For optimal results, super-intensity camera lights were needed.

I found three lights tucked in the furthest corner of the cubicle.

Elaine battled her raging emotions. Then she began to mewl, realizing fully the truth of that night so long ago.

I ran out of the cubicle after her, clutching Elaine in my arms.

Duffy remained behind in the alcove, never looking at Elaine.

"You couldn't have known. There was no way you could have suspected something like this," I offered, hoping somehow to soothe the torrents wrenching inside.

"I think we'd better clear out. If somebody comes now, we'll be in way over our heads. I'll put everything back the way it was," Duffy said.

"Any video tapes in there?" I asked.

"No. Whoever's doing it takes them when they leave."

****

I clung to my newly acquired wealth of information. I had more than I knew what to do with. But none of it was significantly useful to me—yet.

Was there a link between the cabin and Ali's disappearance? Or was the cabin setup just some kind of sick male perversion. Some of these college geeks really got off doing perverted stuff like this.

There was no doubt now that Reid had drugged Elaine, placing her into some kind of somnambulant state—not asleep but not awake either. In such a suggestive state, Reid took advantage of her and videotaped it. But for what end? Show his frat buddies? Sell it as pornography? Use it against Elaine?

None of it made much sense. He was on the tape with her. If the tape became public, it incriminated him.

Back at Ranhurst, Duffy had to return his roommate's car, then study his brains out.

I wanted to talk, needed to verbalize what we had seen. But likewise, I had to prepare for Algebra on Monday.

As Saturday turned to night and the night wore on, fatigue ground away at my concentration. I thought more about the cabin and less about what should have been foremost on my mind, plotting polynomial equations.

I paced. Instinct urged me to cling to my chugging train of thought. Elaine said she took sick after returning from the cabin. For some reason that became important. Important enough that it refused to go away.

Ali. Was Ali sick?

It was late, too late for a telephone call. But I needed answers.

Four rings. No answer.

Six rings.

A sleepy voice answered.

"Beth, Trish. I need to ask something real important." The words raced from my mouth.

Beth's voice grew immediately alert.

"Last term, sometime near the end of March or early in April, were you sick?"

"Was I sick?"

"Yeah, the flu or something like that?"

"No. I had the flu right after Christmas. I missed three days of work, why?"

"Did Ali come home for a weekend around the end of March or early April?"

"No, why?"

"Around that time Ali said she was going home for the weekend because you were sick, and she wanted to be there to take care of you. But you weren't sick?"

"No. What have you learned?"

"I don't know yet. Ali was ill when she came back from that weekend. She just laid in bed and slept. I remember because she didn't eat. I worried about her. I just figured she picked up the same bug you had."

"Trish, what's this all about? You're saying Ali left campus for the weekend, and she told you she was coming home to take care of me."

"Exactly. But she never went home. And when she returned she was sick. Beth, I think I know where she was that weekend."

"Should I come there?"

"No. Just stay where you are. When I learn more, I'll call you."

I hung up the phone unconsciously. Matt Evans lured Ali to that cabin for the weekend. He undoubtedly videotaped her and drugged her the same way Reid had drugged Elaine.

My heart pounded. I chewed at my lower lip.

"Ali, why didn't you confide in me? What happened to you?"

I set another link to Delta Rho in place. What were they doing? How did Ali fit in with these sick creatures?

22

Is The Twenty-ninth Good For You?

Quenby met me as I breached the library doors, and without a word, motioned me to follow him. He led, I followed down to the lower level through the maze of bookshelves and aisles until we reached a corner far removed from the rest of the library.

"I thought you should have a look at this," he said handing me a stack of pages that had been photocopied. The pages on top were faxes, I realized as I began skimming.

"Can you boil this down?"

"Sure, you ever hear of a bloke named Crowley?"

"No."

"Self-proclaimed head of the worldwide Church of Satan."

I suddenly became very interested. A cult.

"So, he's a cult leader?"

"No. Besides he's been dead for quite some time."

"So why are we talking about him?"

"My uncle turned up some writings Crowley set down before he died. Mind you, the guy was considered a crackpot fanatic in every civilized country in the world. But he did organize a huge following of Satan worshippers all over the world.

"How does this tie into us?"

"I'm not sure. In one of his manuscripts Crowley claimed to have found a way to bridge the world of the living with the world of diabolic entities. He described it as a window to the soul, which can be opened under certain specific conditions and through which Satan's minions can partake in the pleasures of the living.

"Again, let me repeat myself. How does that have *anything* to do with us?"

"Probably nothing. I went surfing the Internet and ran across a reference to a Bloodstone in Crowley's writings. What I haven't been able to determine is if the stone is part of a Sabbat ritual, or if it is protection from it. You see, in centuries past, the stones were worn to protect the wearer from evil."

"So are you saying you think Ali somehow got involved with a Satanic cult here at Ranhurst?"

"You know her better than me. But here's the gravity of what I'm telling you. Crowley also mentioned a blood sacrifice that must take place during the Sabbat. He called it a Joining. There's an underground following on the Internet that is convinced Crowley was right. The demons take one of the living back with them, kind of like a trophy or something like that. Some of the writings got really weird at that point, and my uncle and I, we couldn't actually be certain what Crowley was trying to say."

"When would this Sabbat take place?"

"I'm not sure. Crowley believed there were two times during the year when this window could be opened. But he also stated the conditions that had to exist."

"What conditions?" For a brief moment I asked myself why I was being drawn into this preposterous story. How could this have anything to do with Ali? But she did have the Bloodstone, and Quenby did link the Bloodstone to this Crowley creep.

"Crowley believed water was the medium and that the ritual has to take place in a cave."

"Okay, let's for a moment say that this Crowley cult has kidnapped Ali. When would they perform this Sabbat?"

"I don't know. Crowley believed Walpurgis night was one time."

"And that is?"

"The eve of Mayday. I've uncovered some writings detailing horrifying events that took place on Walpurgis night. It's been a long time since I've even thought about this."

"But you said Crowley believed there was a second one."

"Yes, only his manuscript was incomplete, and I couldn't determine exactly when. It seems he eluded in the beginning to a Catholic holyday that is no longer celebrated."

"Okay, but we can find that out. Suppose you're right. Suppose Ali was taken by this cult. They might be holding her in this cave until the time comes to perform this Sabbat."

"Trish, the time may have already come and gone. We may be too late."

For a long moment neither of us spoke.

"These people live and die by a code. Those who betray the code are severely punished. That could be what happened to that Matt kid they found in the creek."

"Then Ali's in grave danger. If we're not too late. Quenby, do you think you can figure out what day this ritual would take place? Is there any way to piece it together?"

"I don't see how. We can't find any more of Crowley's writings. He would have to have documented somewhere when he believed that second day to be."

"Can we backtrack? If we know it's a Catholic holyday, can we check with the church for holydays occurring during August or September. Ali disappeared the last week of August. So it must be a day close to that time."

"Trish, I'll do what I can."

I tried on my walk back to the main lobby to put most of what Quenby had told me out of my mind. I realized nothing he said had to have any shred of truth to it to be important. If the people in that cult believed it was true, they would perform the ritual anyway.

By the time I hit the bright sunlight I had switched my mind back to the matters at hand. But there was something gnawing at the back of mind. I just couldn't figure out what it was and why it persisted so.

23

The Right Place

Duffy and I shared a blanket beneath a majestically arched maple and beech canopy on a hill crest. The heady scent of trimmed grass perfumed the air around us. While I sat crossed-legged, leaning against the bole of a tree, Duffy lay across from me, resting on his elbow, his Biology book open before him. But his eyes were on me. I hoped his mind was forever on me.

Students strolled across the campus lawn, yet we felt secluded, their chatter amounting to nothing more than a whisper on the wind.

In ruminative silence, I focused on Astronomy.

"Duffy, you're not studying," I said without lifting my eyes.

"Sorry."

After a while Duffy noticed my habit of lifting my head—but not to look at him. Hardly a minute passed without me glancing off. At first, he probably dismissed it as nothing more than a need to draw my eyes from the text, but after another three times, it must have sparked his curiosity.

Overhead, bluejays, sparrows, larks and blackbirds fluttered from tree to tree in a playful way. At the time, neither of us took more than a passing interest in the winged denizens.

I shifted onto my side to rest my head on my palm. As I did, Duffy reached across to gently tickle me, his smile puckish and innocent.

I giggled, then pasted on a stone–stern face and returned to my studies.

"No playing, we're here to work," I scolded as somber as possible.

I allowed Duffy sufficient time to return to his book, then I gently leaned over to tickle him under his arm.

"Oh yeah," he lilted, rolling over to trap my arm beneath his weight while at the same moment launching his own feverish playful assault upon me.

I laughed until tears came to my eyes, unable or unwilling, to fend off his determined attack.

"I really do love you," I whispered for only him before he kissed me. As I rolled back, the Bloodstone I had been wearing under my blouse came up from beneath the material. Since learning of the words on the stone, I've been unable to let it off my person.

When we stopped laughing, Duffy kissed me again. A kiss that lingered for a long enduring moment. I wished this were an island that only Duffy and I inhabited and all else was a million miles away.

I slipped my arms under his, pulling him close. Maybe I could retake Astronomy in the spring? Along with Algebra, of course. I had given up hope of passing the class, and we were only three weeks into the semester.

When Duffy eased his lips from mine, I arched my back, holding him in my embrace. I wished to be alone on a sun-drenched beach in a secluded cove off the ocean. I figured an island was too much to hope for. We could make love at this moment without being disturbed or inhibited. The last thing I wanted was to let go. I wished I could stay like this forever. I wanted Duffy always beside me, always with his hand in mine.

We parted reluctantly. Duffy brushed my cheek with a departing kiss, as if circumstance forced us to say good–bye, then drew himself back across the blanket.

"What are your plans after college?" I asked.

"Get a job, any job. My old man can't wait for me to start working so I can pay him back. What about you?"

"Join the FBI."

"Get out of here. You *really* want to join the FBI? I figured that was just some Matlock complex you had."

"Yeah, I do. God knows they could use people who really care. Not like those Fools, Boneheads and Idiots in Cleveland."

Silence settled over us. Time to put dreams and fantasies away and get back to work.

From high in the trees, the birds swooped in like hawks. The bluejays and larks led the attack. The first wave pecked at my face, while a second wave of blackbirds dove toward my chest. My shrieks shattered the otherwise serene air around us. Sparrows glided in low along the ground like attack planes, climbing at the last second to go for my hair.

Duffy launched his book, stretching his body over mine to shield me from the insane onslaught of fluttering wings.

I flailed my arms, screaming when a bluejay went for my hair.

As quickly as the attack came, it ceased. Silence reigned. The birds retreated, climbing to safety high in the leafy canopy.

I sat up and straightened my clothes, shaking off the eerie sensation that the birds were attempting to fly under my blouse. In doing so, the Bloodstone fell back hidden beneath the material.

"What the hell? We trapped in some Alfred Hitchcock movie?" Duffy said, planted defensively and armed with his book, ready to thwart another onslaught.

"Crazy friggin' birds attacked me..." I stammered.

"Why don't we just go. I'm getting hungry anyway," Duffy said, retrieving his scattered papers before the wind could snatch them away.

"No, let's stay a little longer."

"Why?"

Duffy watched as my eyes traced a line toward the westward buildings. The parking garage loomed beyond a maple grove, and closer still, the weathered old Chandler Hall.

"You didn't just happen to pick this place, did you?"

"No."

"That's why you kept looking away."

"I'm sorry. I came here to keep an eye on Chandler Hall."

Duffy stared at the stone building now color-less in the fading light.

"Why?"

"I don't know.... Ali's Walkman was found there. I just wanted to..."

I could find no words to explain the restless churning in my mind. Chandler Hall had some-thing to do with Ali.

"I take it we're staying."

"I don't know. I..."

Duffy kissed me.

"How about I get dinner," he offered with a lover's wink.

His understanding smile both melted me and fueled my guilt. What was I doing, anyway?

"You're really something special."

"So are you," Duffy said. He kissed me again, this time with more than a hint of bottled pas-sion.

I feared he might dump me if he knew why I wanted to come to this place. And why I now had to stay. Obsession forced logic from my brain. Especially since I had no justification for my seemingly wild suspicions. Duffy was anything but your typical self–absorbed, sex–starved college geek. He stood beside me no matter what. If that isn't love, I could only wonder what is.

Not long after Duffy's return, students began shuffling up the walkway toward Chandler Hall. A few dribbled past the old building, ambling on to the parking garage, but most trekked up the stone stairs and through the front doors.

The activity held me spellbound. So much so, that Duffy and I packed up our books and took up residence on a bench ten yards from the building.

"It's getting dark. Classes on the second floor have already begun. I don't know what you're hoping to find, but I think whatever it is, it's either not there or gone."

"Just a while longer. Please..."

Duffy flipped through his book to find his place.

I studied the building, bouncing ideas off the walls the way a kid would bounce a rubber ball. Why Chandler Hall? What reason would Ali have for coming here?

I made a full and careful scan of the area, missing nothing. What would Ali do around here? Or could the Walkman, in fact, have belonged to someone else?

Even I was getting restless. In the still, the faint drone of a lecture drifted out the open windows. Occasional laughter crinkled the air.

By now the sun was a rufous glow over the treetops. Duffy closed his book, as reading became impossible. I had long before abandoned my studies.

A luminescent glow approached on the walkway. At first only the light was discernible. Then the soft click of metal against metal. The sound grew steadily louder, the light more intense.

I watched the light making its way toward Chandler.

Catwoman peddled past with her pedal scrapping the kick stand and the round light on her handle bars penetrating the gray dusk. She coasted, unaware that Duffy and I sat on the nearby bench. Seconds later, darkness swallowed her up.

Square halogen lamps buzzed on over Chandler's front doors, casting the stairs and the neighboring path in silver.

"I really think it's time to go. The mosquitoes are biting," Duffy complained.

I scanned once more.

"You're right. This whole thing was stupid. I'm sorry I dragged you out here for nothing."

"I'd rather be here with you than in my room alone."

"Thanks, I'm sorry."

"No need to apologize. I understand. You need to do something. As long as you're doing something, there's reason to hope. But it's been three weeks. I…"

I put my fingers to his lips. My eyes locked on movement cutting through the penumbra at the parking garage.

Two silhouettes strolled the walkway toward Chandler.

Neither I nor Duffy moved. The night and the surrounding trees cloaked us in darkness.

No words reached our ears. The two silhouettes walked at a pace neither hurried nor unusual. When they approached the steps to Chandler Hall, they came under the spray of light.

I held my breath.

A grim, dark–eyed Kevel and a smileless Simon took the stairs two at a time. A second later, they disappeared inside the building.

"You think that's coincidence?" Duffy whispered.

I shook my head.

Neither of them carried books; I doubted they were there for class.

Again Delta Rho. Ali's Walkman turns up near Chandler. Now Delta Rho shows up.

"Classes should let out in ten minutes. What do you figure they're doing in there now?" I asked.

"I don't know. But I think we'll wait around to find out."

In the pitch still of a moonless night, ensconced in the midst of a bushy copse, Duffy and I knelt in soft earth, vigilant in a task Duffy had yet to fully understand.

Chandler's third floor lights went out. Only the second floor lights burned.

"I really respect you, but I think what we're doing is going nowhere," he said.

Duffy swatted to keep the mosquitoes off his flesh.

"Sshh!" I scolded.

While Duffy trained his eyes on the side doors, I focused on the front steps flooded with light. Through the glass doors I could see part of the empty main corridor.

Clamoring chairs sundered the night still. Moments later students filed out of Chandler in a gushing stream. During the exodus, the second floor lights went dark. From top to bottom, the old building was being put to sleep.

I studied those leaving the building through the front doors. In a crowd, Kevel might be difficult to spot. But not Simon. His towering frame and straw–colored hair marked him even in a crowd.

Duffy watched the few students who left through the side doors. None were Kevel or Simon.

A trickling of students flowed down the path leading across the common, then meandered to the other halls.

I tugged Duffy's sleeve.

"Nothing," he snapped without straying.

Duffy pointed.

I shook my head. After the stream dried up, I settled back in the copse.

"You see them?" Duffy asked, his eyes still vigilant.

"No, you?"

"*Nada.*"

"We missed them. Damn. I'm sure that was Kevel and that other guy from the frat house." I thought for a moment. "So, why were they in there in the first place?"

"This is crazy. Could be a dozen reasons."

"I know. But if they were attending a class, they were extremely late."

"Maybe they came to meet someone. Or talk to a professor."

"Why didn't we see them come out?"

Duffy said nothing. He gazed at the now silent building.

As we picked our way out of the thicket, a uniformed guard climbed the steps. With jingling keys, he threw the lock that secured the building for the night.

****

A Tuesday afternoon trip to a friend who worked in Administration confirmed that neither Kevel Moreland nor Simon Lindstrom were registered for any classes meeting in Chandler Hall. Their purpose, then, for being there had nothing to do with academia, or so it seemed to me.

Duffy knew exactly where we were going when we set out after classes. But this time he came prepared. As dusk approached, he removed a can of OFF mosquito repellent and with great fanfare displayed it to an invisible crowd as if he were the great Houdini.

"Duffy, you do think of everything, don't you?"

"I try."

Safely settled within the shadowy recesses of the thicket, we watched as the scene from the night before replayed itself. *De javu.* The students filed in around seven. Then as the last light of day faded, Catwoman peddled by with her dim round light cutting through the growing darkness. But this time no soft clicking metal sounds preceded her.

Later, against the backdrop of classes in session, and the halogen lights painting the front stairs, and the crickets chittering at their feet, Kevel and Simon made their way up the Chandler Hall stairs.

This time, though, they stopped at the doors while Simon quickly rubbernecked the area. His eyes stopped to stare at the thicket.

We held rock steady behind leafy oleander bushes. Could those two sense our presence? Or we they just being careful?

Duffy squeezed my hand when Kevel and Simon disappeared into the building. This was no longer coincidence.

I felt a rush of excitement mixed with fear racing through me. Was it Duffy's touch or what we had just witnessed? I couldn't decide which.

"So, they're not in there for a class," I whispered.

"How many other reasons can there be?"

In the ensuing silence, we waited. The minutes ticked away. This time I commanded myself to determine which way they headed after exiting the building. Their presence for a second night fueled my speculation. Could Ali have been inside Chandler Hall after her return? Was she passing Chandler Hall on her way to the parking garage when something happened?

I gazed up at the gibbous moon rising over the trees. This Friday was the twenty-eighth— the night the moon reached its climax and the day Matt had marked on his calendar. What had Matt planned for that day?

Students filed out of the building. The first flood burst through the doors as if propelled by some unseen rocketing force. This time Duffy and I remained unwavered in our task. After the last of the crowd drifted away and the building again became silent, I turned to Duffy.

"Nothing," he said, puzzled.

"Me neither. Do you suppose?"

"I don't know."

Duffy watched two professors with briefcases in hand jog down the stairs.

"Let's get inside to look around. If we didn't see them, they're either exiting through a door other than those two, or..."

Duffy and I had no sooner crept free of the copse when the security guard approached. Damn, we had dallied too long. Changing course, we linked hands and strolled past the guard. I glanced back as the guard locked the doors.

"Maybe they're leaving through a door on our blind side?" Duffy said after a while.

"But even so, we'd see them as they moved further from the building. Either way, Duffy, we would still have seen them. Simon's hair and height should have been easy to spot. He's enough of an oddity that we wouldn't miss him in the crowd."

"Agreed. So then what you're really saying is that you don't think they actually came out of the building?"

I looked at Duffy; Duffy looked at me.

"No. Two nights in a row."

"And a dozen mosquito bites later," Duffy added.

"They go in—but don't come out."

"Oh no, it's the Roach Motel!" Duffy said.

We both tried to laugh but knew the ominous meaning behind what we had just witnessed.

"So what do we do? Go to the police?"

"Right now all we've got is a hunch. Besides, nobody's going to believe us. And once we make this public, we may sacrifice our chances of finding out what is really going on."

We walked on in silence for a dozen strides.

"We need a good look around inside Chandler. Can you meet me here tomorrow night, just before dark?" I asked.

"I'll be here..."

I stopped. There was an edge to Duffy's words.

"What?" I asked.

"Promise me you're not, I repeat, not going to do anything until I'm here with you. Do you understand?"

"Understand."

I kissed him, not to seal my word, but because I needed to taste his lips and feel his warmth against me.

Duffy slipped his arms around my waist and held me with such veracity that I thought I would stop breathing.

****

The hour of eight came and went. Still no Duffy. Dusk faded quickly into night. Three times I checked myself after starting for the steps to Chandler Hall. Was it just anxiety or were there more people milling around the building tonight?

Where was Duffy? Time was running short. We needed to get inside Chandler before classes ended and the guard came around to lock the doors.

I waited.

Catwoman peddled by.

"Sorry I'm late. I got hung up," Duffy said on his approach, so as not to startle me.

"It's about time. Let's go."

I led, having cased Chandler Hall's ground floor earlier in the day, and having formulated what I thought was a well-developed plan.

"How long have you been here?"

"Two hours."

"Did they show up?"

"Not yet."

"Let's wait here, go in after them. If we follow them, we could see where they're going once inside," Duffy offered.

I sensed he was more than just a little apprehensive about what we were about to do. And I couldn't blame him, recalling the bruises left on his face by his earlier encounter with Kevel.

"Can't. They know my face too well. I'd be recognized before I got to the front doors."

"You're right."

I sensed Duffy's reluctance. I felt it in the way his hand held mine. In that moment, the blood and bruising from Duffy's last encounter with Delta Rho played across my mind. I looked at him. If only Duffy were taller, more athletic with broader shoulders and bigger arms.

At the fringe of the darkness cast by the trees, I pulled Duffy close, kissed his lips softly.

Duffy slid an arm around my waist and drew my body next to his. He refused to let our lips part until he needed to take a breath.

"Thanks, I needed that," Duffy whispered.

"I did too."

After checking the walkway, we trotted up the steps and disappeared inside Chandler Hall.

At the first intersection of corridors, I stopped, confused.

"Don't tell me we're in here, and now you don't know what to do."

"Okay."

"Okay what?"

"Okay, I won't tell you I don't know what to do."

"Great."

I started down a corridor. Duffy followed.

"What are we looking for?" he asked, seeing my face washed with confusion.

"I'm not sure."

"Okay."

"Well?"

I checked doors on the main floor. All locked.

"All rooms remain locked when not in use. Only professors and administrators have keys. Except for security, they carry master keys," Duffy informed me.

"If all the doors are locked, where do those two go?"

"Beats me. I still say we'd have a better chance of finding that out if we just found a vantage point and waited until they showed up."

"And if they never show up?"

"We spend the night in this haunted old building."

"Why do I get the feeling you'd like that?"

"Because I'm smiling?"

Duffy reversed our trek. We took up a position on the landing between the first and second floors on the staircase just inside the main doors.

"You're sure they didn't enter before I got here?"

"I'm sure. The only way they could have gotten by me is if they entered the building before I arrived."

"And what time was that?"

"A little after six–thirty."

In the gnawing silence, we waited. A lone set of footsteps clicked from down the first floor hall. I edged out to get a look. Duffy eased me back out of sight.

"One person," Duffy said.

"So."

"So, the footsteps are from someone already inside the building. Did you hear the doors closing?"

"No."

"Some FBI agent you'd make."

I sneered in mock anger, then squeezed his hand.

Silence returned. I checked my watch. Another twelve minutes before the classes would adjourn. *If* they held to their schedule. In this heat, they may just let out early.

Outside the sun was gone and the sky had lost its luster. Incandescent ceiling lights provided the only illumination.

"I think..." I started, but Duffy put his finger over my lips.

A second later I heard doors wheeze closed. Two distinct sets of feet invaded the quiet corridors, both squeaking in rubber–soled shoes.

My heart raced. *They* were in the building. Sweat worked its way between our still clasped hands.

"They're on the staircase!" Duffy whispered, pulling me up the stairs to the second floor.

The sounds faded too quickly. They weren't coming up.

"Come on," Duffy commanded, working his way stealthily down to the landing. He inched his face over the railing. From the intensity in his eyes, I discerned that he realized this was no game we were playing. This was real.

The staircase below was empty.

I followed him to the first floor.

"Where are they?"

"They couldn't make it to the next corridor that fast."

Duffy pointed down.

"Stick right behind me," he warned, starting down the stairs.

Above, chairs and feet echoed through the halls. Noise. Noise that muffled our footsteps, but also kept us from detecting any sounds emanating from below.

Duffy descended the remaining stairs two at a time.

I stopped at the bottom stair behind Duffy's outstretched arm.

As he peered into the hall, he caught the heel of a shoe as someone turned down one of the cross corridors thirty feet away and on the right. Duffy was certain he had seen a high–top running shoe.

"Could be them, but I didn't actually see a face."

"Do we go on?" I asked, now confused, and uneasy, feeling the knots of fear choking off my breathing.

Upstairs, the doors banged open with a cascading burst. Students marched out of the building.

"Your call," Duffy said, studying my eyes.

We stared through a moment's pause.

"Let's go on. We need to know for sure if they're in this building."

During that moment my courage strengthened. The next moment it waned.

Duffy took the point, running the distance only to stop before reaching the corridor. His movements, silent, measured and furtive, reminded me of characters I had seen in old war movies. It also instilled in me the seriousness of the situation. Until this moment I never realized I might have to fight.

Duffy turned back with confusion writ across his face. I suspected he was uncertain of what he would do if he came face–to–face with them. No, I think he knew exactly what he would do. Launch an attack and drag them to the floor until I could clear the building. Then he'd run like hell to catch up with me.

He peered down a dim and empty cross corridor. Only a third of the overhead lights were left on. Duffy motioned for me.

"Where did they go?" I asked.

"I don't know. Follow me and do exactly as I say. Exactly," Duffy commanded, leveling a finger.

My heart raged out of control; I needed no further parenting.

The upper floors of Chandler Hall became quiet. The last students had departed.

"There's another corridor on the left. I don't know where it leads, but let's check it out."

"What about these doors?"

I indicated three closed doors between us and the next corridor. Could Kevel and Simon have slipped into one of the rooms? Had they detected a tail on them?

"Very gently check the doors as we go by. Stop me if you come to one that's unlocked."

I exerted just enough pressure on the door handles to turn them slightly. The first two were locked.

Duffy watched as I stopped at the third door. My fingers went out. My heart was a hammer inside my chest. Cold sweat trickled down my face.

Just as I touched the handle, the overhead lights went out, throwing the hall into the void of utter darkness.

I stifled a scream. But remnants of my voice skimmed the silence.

"Damn!" Duffy whispered, reaching out for my groping, outstretched hand.

"The guard's going to lock the door!" I whispered.

"I know. Did you bring a flashlight?"

"No."

"Great. This isn't going to look good on your FBI application."

I wanted to laugh. Fear kept me silent. I tried the door handle. Locked.

"Follow me," Duffy whispered.

With my hand to his shoulder, I moved in response to his body pulling away from mine. Feeling our way along the wall, we entered a crossing corridor in total night. Duffy slid his hand along until he came to a door. He pushed down on the handle. The door opened.

"What are we going to do now?"

"Be quiet!"

"Why? We're alone, aren't we?"

The sound was barely perceptible. The squeak of rubber on waxed floors.

Duffy and I were stationary. Someone else was moving.

"In here," Duffy commanded, pushing me into the room.

"Don't even breathe."

Duffy listened at the door. The sounds grew louder. But not loud enough to indicate someone passing right outside. Duffy surmised the footsteps came from the main corridor now twenty paces back the way we had come. There were no sounds other than irregular squeaks on the floor.

Moments dragged on. Silence returned.

Duffy withdrew a penlight from his pocket, shining the narrow beam onto my face. My eyes were white with fear, my lips colorless.

"You didn't say you brought a flashlight!"

"You didn't ask."

"Why didn't you use it when the lights went out?"

"Because we're not alone. Even a faint beam like this is detectable from thirty yards in sheer darkness. If our friends *are* down here, the last thing I want them to know is that we're right behind them."

"So what do we do now?"

"You got me, Trish. This was your plan, remember."

The beam illuminated our faces. We stared blankly at each other for a time.

Through those brown eyes, I watched Duffy wrestle with his urge to kiss me, to cuddle me in his arms and tell me not to be frightened. But right now there were far more important things to worry about. One was where to go from here?

"I figure we've got two choices. We either search the corridors and hope to find them, or we vacate the building," Duffy said.

"What do you want to do?"

"Leave," we whispered together.

Duffy diffused the beam as much as possible with his hand. Our light extended no more than a foot in front of us. In the darkness, that same faint glow was like a homing beacon to a lost ship. Anyone roaming the corridors would spot it immediately. On the other hand, we encountered no other beam of light on the return trip to the main corridor.

We stopped on the last stair before the main floor. Illuminated EXIT signs over the front doors cast a faint glow down the sleeping corridor.

"The doors are wired," Duffy said, holding me back and pointing out small rectangular sensors installed on the glass panels.

"So what do we do?"

"Opening any door or window triggers an alarm at the security office. At best we've got a minute to ninety seconds before anyone can get here. I hope you run real fast."

"Great. So what are we doing?"

"Give me a minute," Duffy said, peeking out at the night.

I pointed to an EXIT sign at the far end of the corridor.

"The side doors...we go out through there. Less conspicuous and only about twenty yards before we hit the trees," Duffy said.

"Let's hope the guard is sitting in Charlie's right now sucking down a cup of coffee."

Duffy and I crawled down the corridor keeping close to the wall. Duffy kept one eye on the main stairs over his shoulder. If those two were still in the building, where were they? We could only hope our paths would not cross now.

"I'm guessing it's a series alarm."

"And that means?" I asked.

"That means, Patricia, all we have to do is give them a logical explanation for an alarm."

I shrugged, trusting Duffy.

"Start running the moment the door opens. Don't stop until you reach the commons. Do you understand?" Duffy instructed.

I nodded.

"Stay off the path. Go through the trees. Don't stop—no matter what. Even if someone yells for you to stop, don't."

I waited ready at the doors.

"What are you going to do?"

"Hopefully fool the Keystone Cops."

Duffy counted three on his fingers. On three, he slammed down the locking bar and threw the door open. Chandler Hall remained asleep though Duffy knew an alarm was blaring at the Public Safety office.

I rocketed out, wishing for half the speed Ali had. I disappeared into the pitch of a clear night. Crossing the lighted walkway, I became visible for a brief moment.

Duffy followed seconds later. Once outside the building, however, he gave a quick tug to confirm that our exit door had relocked. Then he remained visible beneath the light long enough to take up a hand–sized rock.

Glass shattered.

It lasted only a moment, but to Duffy it must have been an eternity. Now they had a reason for an alarm. Duffy spun around, consuming only a second to search for me. He located my flowing silhouette racing up a rise toward the center of campus.

Taking my right flank, Duffy picked up speed until he reached full tilt. My speed surprised him.

Neither of us stopped to breathe until we were well beyond the Administration building.

And wasting no time to talk, we hurried away,
Duffy's arm around mine, holding my trembling
form.

24

The Dungeonmaster

The next afternoon I filed into the library amongst a crowd with one thing on my mind. Algebra had gone particularly bad and now time was precious to me. I had only a few hours available to spend at the library, and I prayed they might be fruitful.

Quenby rose the moment he saw me emerge from the group dispersing into the library lobby.

"Over here," he said and motioned with a wave.

"Thanks for coming," I said.

"Your message was rather cryptic," Quenby said, reading the concern on my face.

"I know. I was afraid if I didn't mask my real intent, your roommate might show up with you."

"No worry about that, Colin's off chasing another Ranhurst pixie."

"Great. Have you seen Duffy yet?"

"Duffy? No."

I detected Quenby's disappointment. Quenby had read more into my code than I had wanted. He must have thought I wanted to meet him for something other than the business of Ali's disappearance.

"I need to look at the drawings for the campus."

"The drawings?"

"You know, the buildings, electrical lines, things like that. The drawings they used to build this place."

"What for?"

I scanned the breadth of the library main floor until I spotted a secluded corner. Then I led Quenby to the privacy of the nook and set my books down.

"They keep the drawings for the buildings here in the library, don't they?" I asked.

"I'm sure they do. We just have to find them."

"I'm looking for tunnels."

"Tunnels?" Quenby asked, louder than he should have.

I worked my fingers nervously through my hair. Then I set a ruffled paperback titled *The Dungeonmaster* on the table between us.

"What's this?"

"Real life. It's about a kid who turned up missing at a Michigan University. Seems there was a network of underground steam tunnels running between the buildings. Students used them to play Dungeons and Dragons. I stayed awake most of last night reading it."

"You think Ali?"

"I just need to know if any tunnels run between the buildings. Can you help?"

"Sit Trish, I'll see what I can uncover."

Minutes passed. I flipped through my Algebra book, but found myself looking up for Quenby every few seconds. How long can it take to locate the necessary documents? After all, libraries cataloged everything.

Quenby returned empty–handed.

"I can't believe…" I started.

"Come on. Third floor. All the architectural drawings for the campus are kept in one cabinet."

I stopped midway up the staircase and turned to scan the main floor for Duffy. He was nowhere in sight. Again he failed to show up. I wondered what could be so important to delay him this time.

In the Charles Wesley Memorial Room, I waited while Quenby went through the wide thin drawers holding the architectural blueprints. Some were clearly annotated and easily discernible. Others were faded and poorly labeled.

Quenby carefully lifted three drawings showing the utilities layout for the entire campus.

"I don't see any indication of tunnels under the campus. This shows that each building has its own heating plant. So there would be no reason to run steam tunnels between the buildings."

"How about for electric power lines?"

"Overhead."

"There's no underground tunnels connecting the buildings?"

Quenby picked through another drawer laden with blueprints, and after close scrutiny of each, concluded no underground tunnels or passageways existed at Ranhurst.

"Do you think this has something to do with your roommate?" he queried further.

While pacing the room I revealed to Quenby parts of what I had witnessed the night before.

"You think it's linked to Ali's disappearance?"

"Yeah."

"Then why don't you look at the drawings for Chandler," a voice said from the door.

I spun around.

"Duffy!"

"Just a suggestion."

"You scared the bee–gee–bees out of us," Quenby said.

I kissed Duffy on the cheek while Quenby returned his attention to the cabinet. He searched drawer after drawer until he at last came upon the architectural drawings for Chandler Hall.

The ink was barely legible. The paper had moldered and discolored so much that the edges crumbled away when Quenby pulled the sheets out of their storehouse. Wincing, he laid them on a nearby table.

"You any good at reading these things?" I asked Quenby.

"I can understand anything built after about 1950. But these are so old, I'm not sure what some of the notations mean."

Duffy leaned over the table, working his finger along the top sheet.

"Wrong one. Let's look at the next one," he said with such a conviction that neither of us could doubt him.

Both Quenby and I shrugged, then eased the top sheet off the table.

Duffy leaned closer to study the second drawing. He stared at one corner for a long time before lifting his head up. He looked into my eyes.

"Well?" I asked, expecting some revelation to be forthcoming.

"Wrong one. Next."

"This is the last," Quenby offered.

Duffy examined the drawing.

"This isn't it. There must be another."

"These are the only ones in the cabinet."

Duffy began his own search through the drawers. "It must be here somewhere, he muttered more to himself than to us."

"There's one missing for Chandler Hall," Duffy concluded after a meticulous search.

"How can you know that?" Quenby asked.

"Because we don't have a drawing for the basement. There should have been another drawing showing the basement layout."

"We're at a dead end?" I asked.

Our search had already lasted more than an hour; still I knew no more than when I first entered the library.

"Ideas?" Quenby said, breaking the long silence.

No one answered.

"I've checked the land surveys for underground tunnels between buildings," Quenby offered to Duffy.

"And?"

"Nothing. Each building has its own independent heating plant. No tunnels for steam pipes or utilities."

"Makes sense. Chandler Hall is really the only ancient building on campus," Duffy said.

"Well, we might as well pack it in for now. There's nothing else we can gain here."

"Wait. I was in a room on the lower floor of the library. I saw some old drawings just like these on a table," I said.

"What room?"

"One with a NO STUDENT ACCESS sign on it."

"Great," Duffy sighed.

"No problem. Allow me. You just lead the way," Quenby offered.

Duffy and I waited at a table near the restricted door. Quenby returned a few minutes later with an excited assistant librarian in tow. She hesitated when it came to unlocking the door, looked around before putting the key into the lock, and reaffirmed that she could get into trouble if anyone found out.

Somehow Quenby's smile and wink quelled all her objections. I suspected there was a story behind Quenby and this young vivacious assistant librarian.

I went right to the table. Exactly as I had seen previously, tattered architectural drawings were on the table.

"Are any of these what we need?"

Duffy peeled back the lower right hand corner of the sheets one at a time. The wait gnawed at my already dangling nerves.

"No. They're all for Wesleyan Hall."

"Paula, are there any more of these drawings around the library?" Quenby asked.

"There's some real old ones under here. We're afraid to handle them for fear they'll come apart in our hands."

Duffy and Quenby found exactly what they were hoping for in the cabinet against the far wall. The basement layout for Chandler Hall stared them in the face.

Without removing the blueprint, Duffy confirmed we had the correct one. Neither Quenby nor I knew what we were looking at, but within a minute Duffy saw it. He never pointed to it, nor did his eyes remain on it for long. But I could see the way his jaw tensed that he had discovered something on that old drawing.

"Okay. I've seen enough. We can go."

"What did you see?"

"Everything is normal. A standard layout. Nothing unusual."

"Oh great, still nothing," I said.

Paula locked the door then whispered something only Quenby could hear. He smiled at her before she left. There sure was a story behind those two.

"Thanks for all your help, Quenby. Sorry we came up empty," I said as we walked back through the lobby.

"At least we tried."

Duffy and I descended the library steps, then turned in the direction of Charlie's. When no invitation seemed forthcoming, Quenby walked off in the opposite direction.

"There *was* something on that blueprint," Duffy said when we were alone.

"There was? I knew it! What?"

"I can't be completely certain of it. But it appears that Chandler Hall was built with a subbasement."

"A subbasement?"

"The basement level drawing showed an access point to a lower level in the building."

"But I've been down there. I spent all afternoon trying to figure out what those two were doing down there. I went completely through the lower level. The only staircases lead up to the main floor.

"My guess is that it was a storage basement, or a bomb shelter or something like that. They probably walled over the access years ago."

"But the access still exists? I mean there is still a basement below where we were last night?"

"There could be. If they bricked it up, then no. But if they didn't..."

"That would explain why those two go in and not come out."

I stopped Duffy on the path.

"Duffy," my voice teetered on fear's edge, "could they have taken Ali there?"

25

Join The Party

Friday. Classes let out for the weekend. Most students kicked back, getting a quick start on the two days off. Even a weekend of Calculus, Chemistry, or debits and credits had its own rewards. Parties, football, intimate moments between lovers. Or at the very least, sleep, glorious sleep.

I, however, focused on one thing as Duffy and I pushed through the double doors of Public Safety. I opposed Duffy's whole idea and was doing this only to demonstrate that my suspicions about Merrifield were on target. Duffy was the one who insisted we go to Merrifield. I had more than just doubts.

Duffy asked politely to see Captain Merrifield. I demanded it.

The officer behind the counter glanced toward the captain's office, then waved us through the gate to Merrifield's secretary.

"We'd like to see Captain Merrifield, if we could," Duffy asked, always trying to be nice and polite.

The prunish secretary gazed blankly over her bifocals. Then she cast her eyes askance to the wall clock.

"Is it *imperative* you see him today?"

"Yes ma'am. This is Patricia Van Worten. She's the roommate of the missing..."

"We know who she is," Merrifield called out from his office as if it took great effort. "I'll see them."

"I just want some information," I announced even before we were in the room.

"You have two minutes."

I sat directly across from Merrifield. Duffy pulled a chair next to mine, much to Merrifield's dismay. Sitting meant we expected more than the proffered two minutes.

Conrad lit a cigarette and busied himself with papers on his desk. I guess he expected the cigarette smoke might accelerate our departure.

"I understand your men found a Walkman a week or so ago on campus," I said.

"A what?"

Merrifield blew his smoke upward, hinting exasperation. He purposely stopped what he was doing to look at me.

"A portable tape player, you know, the kind with the earphones."

"I know what they are. Why?"

"I just thought maybe, well, could it belong to Ali?"

Merrifield wiped the sweat from the back of his neck before answering. I guess in a gesture of intolerance.

"I understand how you feel. I'm sure you and Althea were good friends. I'm also sure you feel slighted that she left without telling you."

"Look, I just want to know if maybe that player belongs to Ali," I injected with a caustic resonance in my voice.

Duffy gently covered my hand. He seemed to remain so calm even though I knew what Merrifield was doing.

Merrifield caught the gesture.

"It's just a garden variety tape player. Kids lose them all the time."

"Can I see it? Ali was meticulous. She would have marked it for identification purposes. If it belongs to Ali, I'll know. It's a yellow Sports Walkman."

"Hell, I don't even know if it's still around."

"But your men would have checked it thoroughly for identifying marks, wouldn't they?"

Merrifield rose stiffly. He sucked on his cigarette, turned his head askance, expelling the smoke toward the floor as he stormed out of the office. I could see we had taken his patience to the limits. But I didn't care, since I am now suspicious of anything that comes across his lips.

"What are you doing?" Duffy blurted in a nervous whisper.

"Trust me. If he checks out, I'll tell him."

"Trish," Duffy said, with more of a paternal ring than I was willing to tolerate.

"I will."

A minute elapsed. Merrifield returned with an overstuffed clipboard.

"A Sony Walkman was claimed three days ago by Michael Lambert. It's no longer here, and it undoubtedly didn't belong to your roommate."

"Was it a yellow Walkman? Was there a tape in it?" I fired off my questions as if it were obvious I distrusted him.

"I don't know."

"Couldn't there have been another one?"

"No. Says here that one was found ten days ago by our officer. We don't advertise what we find around campus. If someone comes in asking about a lost item, we match their description to what we have on hand."

"Where was it found?"

"Says here by the steps of Reynolds Hall."

"And you're sure it's not Ali's. She had a tape player. I think it was a Sony, too."

"I'm sure."

I rose abruptly and backed out of the office.

Duffy needed no prodding. He quickly followed, shrugging his shoulders in mock confusion to Merrifield. Or maybe his confusion was genuine?

Merrifield returned to his desk, bewildered by the whole exchange.

"I told you," I whispered as we exited. "The Walkman I saw was found near Chandler Hall, except Merrifield doesn't want us to know that. You really think someone came in to claim it?"

"No. But let's find out for ourselves."

"I've got a better idea. You get over to Admin and check with Jeanie. I'm going over to Chandler Hall. I'll meet you there."

26

The Lion's Den

The wait seemed endless. I paced in the trees
a short distance from Chandler's front door.
Then I remembered the letter I picked up earlier
in the day and pulled it from my pocket. I had to
move out of the shadows to catch as much of the
fading sun as possible in order to read the letter.
My friend Ellen was writing again to brag about
her latest steady, a recent transfer to Purdue.
God, he was gorgeous! This time she included a
picture of them arm-in-arm in her dorm room.
She wore a tight t-shirt, and he was wearing a
navy blue jersey with a duck coming through a

arch. I stared at the photo as if it were supposed to mean something.

"You were right. Jeanie checked the records. There's no Michael Lambert registered on campus," Duffy said as he approached.

I slipped the picture and letter hastily into my pocket.

Merrifield had concocted a quick lie. But for what purpose? His attitude only confirmed my suspicions that he was somehow involved with this whole mess.

We advanced on our objective. Chandler Hall's main corridor lay silent, save for the faint sounds of Duffy's and my footfalls. Above, a second-floor class on ancient artifacts was still in session. Outside, dusk surrendered to night.

The first glimmer of the full moon rose behind the jagged colorless skyline. The night of the twenty-eighth began. The night of the climactic moon.

My heart pounded. Inside, fear taunted me; my palms were sweating. I reached out to Duffy, drew strength that his hand was there. Something inside kept urging me to back out of this now. I knew I couldn't listen to that voice of reason. I knew Delta Rho was involved in Ali's disappearance and Delta Rho was inside this building.

Twenty minutes earlier we had watched Simon enter the building alone. Minutes after that, I saw another Delta Rho enter. Neither came out.

Shortly after that Duffy and I entered Chandler Hall. Something was drawing us to its core. Something neither of us at the moment understood.

Duffy led the way to the basement. The air was cooler, still. No other sounds bobbed to the surface. Measuring each step, and using the fringes of the first floor EXIT sign's light, we advanced down the corridor. Only when we were certain it was safe, did we risk switching on the penlight Duffy carried.

"So where did they go?" I whispered. A preliminary search turned up no human presence in the basement.

"Are we sure they're even still here?" Duffy asked, his face outside the flashlight's weak glow.

"They didn't leave this building. I'm betting they didn't leave the building the other night, either."

"Okay, so where do we go from here?"

Duffy knew the answer, but he needed further convincing it was the best course to follow. He hesitated, then gravitated toward the building's center. Visualizing the blueprint, Duffy followed one of the corridors to the far end.

I tugged slightly on each door we passed. All locked.

Overhead, classes let out. Duffy and I stopped when the sounds of closing doors and clattering footsteps reached us.

"They'll be locking up and setting the alarm," Duffy whispered.

The overhead lights came on. A guard's footsteps descended the steps.

"He's making a walk–through," Duffy whispered.

Duffy and I backtracked the way we came, searching for somewhere to hide. In the distance the footfalls grow more distinct.

At the last second, Duffy drew me into a darkened corner beneath a staircase. The sudden jerky movement knocked the letter and photo from my pocket to the floor. I had to leave it. Chest–high cardboard cartons afforded concealment, enough that if we remained motionless, and the guard didn't poke around, we might go undetected.

Neither of us breathed while the security officer ambled through the corridor. We waited for the sounds to dissipate.

I reached out and retrieved my fallen things. Duffy glanced at the picture. I stared at it.

"Where'd you get that?" he asked.

"A friend at Purdue. Look at the jersey. What's that duck jumping through a hoop all about?"

"You don't know? You really don't know?"

"No. Should I?"

"That's not a hoop. That's the letter O. For the University of Oregon. Why?"

The overhead lights went out.

"It's just us and them now," Duffy whispered in a voice that struck fear into my soul, though I'm sure he didn't mean it to.

I remained silent. The University of Oregon? Why is that all of a sudden making my stomach convulse. Wait a minute. Nick said they lost a girl at the University of Oregon. *Us against them,* I thought. Duffy's history of confrontation with Delta Rho failed to muster confidence.

We dog-trotted, retracing our path to the point where the guard had forced us into retreat. We proceeded cautiously behind the flashlight's beam.

"The building plans originally showed a stairway access to the subbasement somewhere around here."

"Are you sure?"

"How can I be sure? The building plans could have been wrong. We could have turned down the wrong corridor."

Duffy raked his weak beam along the top of the wall. Nothing.

"What are we looking for?"

"Anything that might indicate a walled–over staircase. Variations in paint color or newer-looking wood trim. The only other way to find it is to measure exact distances from the blueprint."

"Great, so what do we do now?"

"I don't know, you're the junior detective, or should I say apprentice G–man."

"Very funny, Duffy. But if *we* can't find it, how could someone else have found it?"

"Good point."

Duffy backed up, both in mind and body, and rethinking our position, he chose an alternate corridor.

"You know, we could be doing this all night. I wish you had a better idea..." I started.

Duffy stopped me mid–sentence with a squeeze to my hand.

"Let me think for a minute. This way."

We flowed to the end of the corridor.

I moved around him with a startling sense of urgency.

"Trish, wait."

We faced two doors on adjoining walls. The first door was locked, the second unlocked.

Duffy angled the beam at the lock mechanism. The mechanism was jammed—the door became impossible to lock.

Inside, Duffy swept the beam across a row of mops and brooms, a dusty old circular floor buffer and a deep sink. To one side, a five–tier shelf unit held cans and bottles of cleaning agents and polishes.

Duffy crossed to the sink and turned on the faucet.

A tremoring thud hammered overhead.

I jumped, swinging my arm into Duffy's, which caused him to drop the penlight.

The light immediately died.

"It's just old pipes. Don't be so skittish. The sink is for real, anyway."

"Sorry. It scared me."

"Yeah, it also put an end to our light," Duffy said shaking the small flashlight.

"Bulb's gone."

"You bring a backup?"

"No. Did you?"

"No."

We stood in the darkness listening to each other's breathing.

"Duffy, could this be where the staircase would be?"

"You think it's coincidence the door to this janitor's closet is jammed?"

"No."

Duffy struck a match. The bulbous saffron light painted our faces. I had to swallow an irresistible urge to reach across and kiss him. I was that scared. No, I was totally consumed with fright.

"There's got to be something here," we said in unison.

"Start searching."

"No, wait a minute, Trish," Duffy said, his voice for the first time insistent, while his hand tightly clinched my elbow.

"What if we find something? We're going to need professional help."

I freed my elbow and ran my fingers along the sink.

"Promise me if we find something, we're going to get out of here and get help," he added.

"Right. Check the shelves. You want me to call Merrifield? We're supposed to rely on him? Tell him we think we know what's going on?"

"No, I want you to call in the FBI."

"Oh, and that from the one that originally said the FBI stands for Fools, Boneheads, and Idiots."

Duffy dropped his nearly spent match and lit another. I directed the flickering light to the seams of the walls.

In the marginal light, all appeared proper. This place was nothing more than a janitor's closet. But when I had Duffy sweep the match close to the floor, we detected long scrapings that marred the concrete.

And a rush of air bent the flame.

I kicked aside a bucket on castors. Positioning the match an inch above the floor, I studied the markings. Running my fingertips along the ridges, I came away with a white powdery residue.

"Feels like plaster."

The scrapings disappeared beneath the wall.

Duffy dropped the match. The seeping air extinguished the flame.

Returning to my feet with the help of Duffy's arm, I began a meticulous search along the seam of the back wall. I pushed hard against the side. Nothing happened. I worked my way along, feeling for a lever or latch that might hold the wall in place.

"Look Trish, this isn't like in the movies. Ouch!" The match burned Duffy's fingers.

"You're not going to find a..." Duffy stopped when I pushed on the opposite corner. The wall separated slightly at the seam.

"This is a doorway...to the staircase!"

Duffy struck another match, took a quick inventory of those remaining, then stepped in beside me. Together we worked our hands along the seam. Still, we found no way to force it open. But something had to be holding the wall in place.

Duffy turned the feeble light over to me. He grabbed onto the hooks suspending the mops and brooms. He pushed hard.

Nothing.

He lifted with a weightlifter's grunt, still nothing. In frustration, he pulled the hooks toward him.

Click!

Something on the other side unlatched. The seemingly innocuous wall now rotated with ease about a center axis.

Fetid stale air, thick with raw earth, assaulted our noses. But we detected something else rising out of the stench. Something familiar, though I, at first, failed to identify it.

I felt an icy premonition of death invade my soul. This was a *bad* place. I knew in that instant I would descend that staircase to the depths below. Something more powerful inside me had begun to rise.

27

Rendezvous With Destiny

"You know what's down there?" I whispered. A gale force of terror swept into me, causing goose flesh to rise everywhere. The hairs on my arms were on end. I stared blankly into the lightless abyss.

"Yeah...Ali," Duffy uttered. His voice had taken on a fearful utterance. His eyes never strayed from the black void.

The impotent light of a dying match illuminated no further than the first stair of a decrepit

stone staircase descending into the miasma below. A whisper urged us to enter.

"I'm going down there. Ali's down there."

"No, Trish. We don't know *what's* down
there."

"The Delta Rhos are down there. They've got
Ali."

"Maybe we better back off, get help," Duffy
said.

"Yeah, like campus security? Duffy, for all
we know they're part of this."

Duffy held my arm. I searched his eyes in
that moment. I expected to find cowardice. Yet I
detected something else.

"If I go for help, promise me you'll wait here?"
Duffy asked. He already knew the answer. He
knew there was no turning aside now.

"I'm going down there. I'm going to find Ali,
and I'm bringing her up."

Duffy tightened on my arm; he probed deep
into my eyes. He saw only courage in my glistening blue orbs. I don't know if that was what
spurred Duffy's courage or if something else has
risen from deep inside him.

"Let's call that FBI agent you talked to. He'll
come here. He'll..."

"There's no time."

"Okay, Trish."

Duffy became very calm. Something I didn't
expect nor knew how to interpret. He unscrewed
a broom head from its staff while I watched.
Then he measured the stick across his hands.

"I go first," he said, striking another match
and launching that first step into the unknown.

"No argument from me."

Not without trepidation we crossed that first uncertain stair, descending into the bowels of the edifice. We stopped four steps into our journey.

"What's that odor?" I asked.

We paused again a half dozen steps before reaching the subbasement floor.

"I know that smell."

Duffy stopped me at the bottom of the staircase. In the flickering light, he spotted a splintered old axe handle; a few paces further, he picked up a burlap sack. Combined, we now had a torch and sufficient light to proceed. The flickers of yellow light danced across the crumbling stone walls that flanked our right.

I felt an icy shiver pass through me. It struck terror in my heart. Something stirred deep inside. It was as if something had awakened from a dormant state and began to stretch. What I didn't realize was that it would soon be fully awake.

"There's something you should know, Trish."

"I think we should follow that wall."

"Trish, wait a minute."

"What?" I yelled, breaking my whisper.

"I'm not who you think I am."

I froze. What was he intimating and why now?

I read Duffy's eyes in the flickering light. What was he saying? The words held me. Was he one of them? My hands trembled and I started putting a measure of distance between us.

"I'm not a student at Ranhurst. I'm an undercover DEA agent."

I stopped moving.

"Yeah right, Duffy. Nice try. I've seen you in action, remember? The fight at Delta Rho, you didn't come across..."

"Listen. My real name is James William MacDuff. Not Duffy Wentworth. I'm a special agent out of San Francisco."

"Duffy, I think it's great you telling me you're Superman, and there's nothing to worry about. Let's just find Ali and get out of here."

"I'm serious. I was sent here to find Ali. I'm on Nick Logan's task force."

"Okay fine, Duffy. You're a DEA agent. Great, at least now we have gun. You do have a gun?"

"No gun."

"Candle wax," I blurted.

We stood near the staircase. The scurrying sounds of unseen creatures just beyond our light reached our ears.

"No gun! What kind of agent are you?"

"I think a gun would have blown my cover, don't you?"

"Someone's burning candles down here. Duffy, the ritual. The Sabbat as Quenby called it. It's tonight. The twenty-ninth is the Feast of Michaelmas. That's why they're burning candles."

"No, they're burning candles because there's undoubtedly no electricity down here."

"Nick said the family of that missing girl in Texas burns candles on eve of the Feast of Michaelmas. Tonight. That was the night their daughter disappeared. Don't you see?"

"Trish, you're jumbling everything together. You're not making sense. Don't let all this hokey stuff get to you. We need to concentrate on finding Ali, okay? And remember, we just look around and if we find anything suspicious we back out of here and get help."

"Don't you understand? There's no time. We have to get to Ali now."

A wide straight corridor ended at a set of rotted doors thirty paces distant. Overhead, new wood reinforced century–old beams.

Hoisting the torch, Duffy scanned the breadth of the space before us. Six–foot crates lined our left. They must have been decades old. Jagged water lines, four feet above floor level, crossed each.

"I don't understand?" I said.

"Don't understand what?" Duffy responded without looking back.

"If you're an agent, and I'm not saying I believe you, then why are you involved with me?"

"Our task force has been trying to nail the guy who took Ali. She isn't the first."

"That's what Logan meant when he said he would be behind me on this."

"Yes."

"Why didn't you tell me sooner?"

"We couldn't risk spooking the guy. It's a very delicate situation."

"So that night we had together?"

"I'm sorry. That wasn't supposed to happen. Not part of the job."

"You're sorry? *You're sorry!*"

"Trish, I didn't plan on falling in love with you. I just couldn't help it."

"Now look, Duffy, you want to jerk me around with your FBI thing, fine. But don't..."

Duffy stopped me.

"It's DEA. Did you hear something?"

We stopped at the first door.

"Wait before you open it."

Duffy handed over the torch and leveled the staff across both hands.

"The DEA teach you how to fight with broom sticks?"

"No. A Koji master did."

Duffy nodded. I opened the door.

The door flopped from its hinges when I pulled. We both jumped back, Duffy poised for a fight. The torch poured light into an empty, web–infested room.

"How old are you?" I asked, realizing I had been assuming all along that he was my age.

"Twenty-five."

"Get out of here. Really? I'd have guessed twenty."

"That's why I infiltrate the campuses where the girls disappeared."

Duffy led me further into the darkness.

"You never asked me how I came by your backpack after that night you lost it on campus."

"So."

"So, didn't you ever wonder what happened to those guys who were after you?"

"You?"

"Me. I remembered you had a lab that night, and I was going to meet you at the bus stop to walk you back to your room. I was late. By the time I got there, the bus had already left. I saw you in the distance and was about to run to catch up when something flashed in the trees. They were stalking you on a parallel course."

"You really were there!"

"Yeah. When I realized there was more than one, and you were the prey, I crept up from behind and took them out before they could get to

you. By the way, you would have been more ef-
fective keeping the backpack instead of throwing
it."

"I didn't throw it, it slipped out of my hand."

I pointed to where the corridor turned to the
right.

"Who were they?"

"Don't know. They took off after my first
strike."

"You think they were Delta Rhos?"

Duffy shrugged.

"You know what I think? I think that cabin
Elaine took us to exposed the 'how' of the selection process," Duffy said.

"Selection process?"

"Yeah. We never could figure out why certain
girls were being singled out. I mean, why one girl
instead of another? These were not random acts
of kidnapping. They were well planned and exe-
cuted criminal conspiracies."

"Conspiracies?"

"Of course. In each case more than a single
person seemed to be involved. There's one man
orchestrating it, but he uses local people around
him to help him carry out the act."

"That's it! Matt and Reid. Of course. They
videotape the girls involved in various sex acts at
the cabin. That's why Ali and Elaine were
drugged. Then they send the tapes down to
Colombia to solicit interested buyers."

"Exactly. The druglord picks the girl he
wants based on her performance, and their man
up here then snatches the girl and keeps her on
ice until they could get a courier to transport her
to Colombia."

"We're saying they selected Ali long before she arrived back at school. And that means Matt had to be the one to get Ali to come back early," I said.

"And their plan would have worked, had they not overlooked one little detail."

"And that is?"

"You. They never factored in Ali's roommate being this tenacious. They probably figured the authorities would think Ali just buckled under the pressure and took off."

"That's exactly what Merrifield said to Ali's parents. You think he's involved?"

"I never place anybody above suspicion. We're talking significant dollars here. And that includes your friends Colin and Quenby."

"How much do they go for?"

"You don't want to know."

"Yeah, I do. What's a woman worth these days on the black market?"

"The girl from the University of Oregon went for a hundred fifty thousand. She turned up dead along with our informant in Cartagena. Both were brutal slayings. We're not going to let it keep happening."

We had come to another door. This one was newer, displayed signs of use. The light fell on a dust free handle and oiled hinges.

Duffy motioned me. I didn't move. It was as if a flash went off inside my head.

"Duffy. Oh my God, Kevel wore a University of Oregon jersey. You lost a girl from there."

"What? When? Where?"

"In a photograph on Matt's desk. Matt, Kevel and Simon were together in a room. Kevel had that jersey on. That's why the goofy duck kept plaguing me."

"No. Goofy's the dog. Donald's the duck. Are you sure?"

"I'm sure."

Another terrifying piece fell into place.

I opened the door and poked the torch in.

This room was unoccupied—but not empty. Our light settled on a table and chair. Crumpled food wrappers and Mountain Dew cans littered the floor. Ali drank Mountain Dew like water. They held her down here. I knew it as if I had witnessed it with my own eyes.

I swept the light left to right.

"The chair," Duffy said, lowering his staff.

Slashed nylon ropes hung off the arms. Rope coils lay on the floor like sleeping snakes.

Duffy ran a finger over the seat. No dust.

"She *was* here, wasn't she?" I said.

Dropping to one knee, I sifted through the refuse. A long pink tail scurried to safety beneath a low shelf.

"They held her down here."

Duffy examined the food stuffs left behind on the table. Bread crumbs—fresh. Chicken fat on the surface—fresh. Whoever was in this room had recently eaten, within hours Duffy muttered to himself.

"Looks like they at least fed her," he offered in a whisper.

We were assailed by the fetid stink of human excrement all around. I fought down the rush of tears clouding my eyes. My God how could they have done this to her.

The bastards! The scream flooded my head but remained internal.

The stench in this place proved so foul it forced me to retch. How could they have held her here? What kind of sick perverted goddamn motherfucking bastards were these freaks. I wanted to scream so badly that I thought my lungs were about to burst. They kept her here under these conditions for who knows how long.

Duffy reached out to me.

"Don't lose it on me now, Trish. I need you strong."

He swatted the ropes off the chair.

"Come on. She's not here now. For all we know, she could be long gone," he said.

"So where are *they*?"

Duffy moved back into the corridor.

At the far end of the narrow hall, two more rotted doors faced us.

"By the tracks, I'd say they're through there."

Our torch cast sufficient light along the brick floor to discern that more than one had traveled that way.

Ahead, pooled water cast an inky glint across the floor. What was it Quenby had said about the Bloodstone? Water was the medium. The medium for what? Suddenly I was having a difficult time thinking. It was if some entity I was incapable of understanding had stepped in to block my memory. There was something bad about the water, but now I could not muster the memory to recall it.

"There must be an underground water source running through here. That could be why they reinforced it, then sealed it off."

"Somebody found a use for it."

"Do we go on?" Duffy asked.

I answered by sloshing through the puddle heading for the doors. Duffy hurried to catch up.

I no longer held on to my hope that Ali was down here and still alive. They had taken her. They had killed Matt. They were beyond the doors.

A part of me screamed to retreat from this place. Find sanctuary in the above–ground world, the world of the living. But a deeper, darker part of me propelled me closer to the huge doors. A silent part was now suddenly awakening. I watched my feet and hands moving and knew exactly where I was going. Yet, there was no way I could change the course the thing inside me had now chosen. Out of nowhere the face of the satyr appeared in my mind's eye. I stifled a scream. Duffy took my arm. Was I entering a nightmare?

I watched my hand go out for the twisted handle on the right side door. I felt my heart hammering inside; my mind reeled. An acid fear eroded my courage.

Behind me, the torch began to fade.

Duffy stopped long enough to rekindle the flame with the last scrap of burlap from his pocket.

I hesitated. The door handle was icy cold and wet. Water seeped into my shoes. I stopped when the rusted creak screeched through the still air.

Duffy readied his staff.

Through the slight crack, the overpowering scent of wax permeated our noses. Then we heard the faint rendering of intoning voices. Many voices all singing in unison, using words foreign to me.

"They're through there," Duffy said.

I eased the door open just enough for both of us to slip through. Our light flickered against crumbling stone walls.

"Trish, promise me we're just going to look for Ali and get out of here."

"I promise."

I moved down the hall until I came to a door on my left. The curved handle resisted my efforts, but not from any locking mechanism, rather from age and unwillingness to function.

A push released the door.

Duffy stood ready despite the fact that his fists and a broom handle were his only weapons.

The chamber was devoid of life. Along one wall old crates and boxes lined halfway up to the ceiling. Directly across from us, ten paces distant were another set of timber doors like the ones we had passed through earlier.

The voices, along with a thin sliver of light, escaped through the gap between the doors. I lowered the torch.

"What do we do now?"

Duffy had his doubts. Was I prepared for what I might find?

We stood stone–still at the doors, peering through the seam at the changing sliver of light. Someone was moving about inside.

From within, the voices continued to drone.

"*Asmodeus erus meum animus esse tuus.*"

"Trish, let's back off."

I moved very slowly toward the doors. Those inside were unaware that Duffy and I had uncovered their secret place. Surprise was on our side.

28

Welcome

I seized the cool handle. Overcoming the weight of the door, I began a slow tedious pull. The mass of aged timber obeyed me smoothly, quietly. The hinges on this door had been greased and worked.

Flickering light gushed through the crack; hushed proselyte voices sifted through the air.

I held my breath. I peered into an angular room with flaming candles latticed against one wall. To the left of the lights, I spied a defiled statue of a crucified Jesus cradled in Mary's arms. Black blood dripped from the statue in the eerie light. A garishly painted Blessed Mary

looked down upon the robed bodies chanting
with their backs to the door. They had removed
Mary's arm and duct–taped it in such a way that
it appeared she was holding on to Christ's pri-
vates.

An unmoving form in a long white and silver
cloak stood before the statue leading their
chant.

"*Asmodeus erus meum animus esse tuus.*"

The words echoed; words, at first, foreign to
me.

Then a woman in nun's habit rose to kneel
beside the cloaked one in prayer. I scanned the
breadth of this bizarre congregation. Seated on a
chair facing at a right angle to the man was
another woman, also clad in shabby habit.
When she lifted her head, vacant eyes stared
unknowingly at the light.

Ali!

I gasped, stifling my noise with a hand to my
mouth.

Duffy peered in, soaking in the entire scene
in that brief moment. Eight of them including
the women. He locked on one with his arm in a
cast, realizing this was the one whose arm he
broke that night in the commons. He must have
in that moment planned a strategy for getting Ali
out, because there was no hesitation nor confusion in his voice or his eyes.

I repeated the words the one before the
statue issued over and over. I had heard them
before. Repetition had rekindled my memory.
The Latin words from the Bloodstone.

The gathering resembled a church service.
People huddled in secrecy to worship behind
closed doors.

The lighted candles, the man upon the makeshift altar wearing a church vestment, the statue of Jesus and Mary elevated before the host of worshippers intoning their words of praise and adoration, all held fast my attention.

Their voices rose in excitement.

Duffy's eyes followed my gesture.

Ali sat motionless in her chair, her lips colorless and unmoving, her blankly gazing eyes slick as if coated with ice. They stared unknowingly into the tongues of flame across from her.

The man turned to face the nun still on her knees beside him. She twisted her body to face him while hoisted her skirt up around her waist.

I saw the profile of the face—Kevel.

Slowly he slid his hand inside his vestment. His face turned resplendent with excitement, his eyes fired in crimson. He unleashed his intumescent phallus for the one kneeling before him.

The nun reached to take him, working his offering between her hands as she began to chant those Latin words. During those moments her voice changed into an ethereal lament, and I knew she was no longer the same.

I reeled from the sight of their vile act. But something inside prevented me from taking my eyes off the one before the mock altar.

Behind the two before the statue, another rose from a bench. As his hood fell, Simon approached the altar. He wore priest's garb beneath his cloak. He turned to profile. He was rubbing himself vigorously, reaching to fondle the now exposed flesh of the kneeling girl.

"Asmodeus erus meum animus esse tuus."

A nerve–shattering shriek crackled through the chant in the chamber. Then a piercing wail resounded. Sounds that came not from this earthly place, but from a diabolic world beyond.

I watched in terror. My heart stuttered.

Kevel's face stretched and contorted, bubbling hideously before turning scabrous and scaly; his skin took on the hue of blood. His eyes glassed over with iridescent green slits. At the same time, his entire mass thickened into something beyond a normal man's nature. An evil licking tongue lashed out from a snarling rictus as below, the nun accepted the gift her idol thrust upon her.

A third man leapt up, writhing like a grisly creature. He crossed to Ali still sitting complacently in the chair. She offered no opposition to his pawing, instead she rose, allowing him to strip her robe.

"I am Jesus of Nazareth," the man warbled, driving his head into her exposed mound.

I pulled myself from the crack at the door.

"Oh my God," I whispered.

Duffy replaced me at the seam, his mind working frantically to find a way to get Ali out. What he witnessed had stripped him of his courage and faith in his ability.

Kevel howled like some lusting beast as he rocked to the motions of the mock nun on her knees before him. Through slimy slitted eyes, Kevel watched with demonic satisfaction as the girl struggled to perform the desecration he demanded of her.

As if approaching to take communion, another dressed in black knelt behind the nun at the altar. He, too, sought to partake in the riches of the evil overwhelming them.

The words turned from Latin to English, spoken with a demon's rasp and spit.

At that moment, the green slits rose from the nun below and cast themselves toward the Christ statue before them. The creature opened its mouth to eject a stream of white slime upon the symbol as if it were ejaculating.

Then, with a sudden jerk of realization, Kevel's head spun around in freaky birdish fashion toward the doors.

Duffy, too terrified to move, hoped this monstrous thing staring directly at him would fail to comprehend what it now saw.

I felt my insides wrench, erupting like an explosion into my throat. The violent thrust forced me back against the wall for support. My heart in violent upheaval, my mouth became as dry and as coarse as desert sand.

Something swept through me like a gale wind, forcing its way deep into my lungs and spreading throughout my insides. I stood helpless to oppose it. It unleashed a power I could not even comprehend, let alone fend off. An invasion had begun.

I felt its icy grip inside, consuming me and seizing domination. I was helpless to oppose it. It came from a place no man could defy. I must yield to its demands.In the darkness, my eyes were stripped of blue and reborn in slime–green slits. My hands curled against my will into wretched, demon claws. My throat bubbled as something spread from deep within. A thick bovine tongue slavered out of my gaping mouth to slash back and forth across my face.

"You *motherfucker!*" a strident demon voice launched from the very core of my throat. I had heard that voice before. I had felt this thing inside me in the past.

Duffy whirled around. Claws clamped the base of his neck. He stared into eyes that could only exist in his blackest nightmare. I witnessed the terror erupting inside him when he looked into what moments ago had been my eyes.

Inside the room, the voices stopped.

"I'm going to fucking kill you!" it said, using my mouth and vocal cords, but something other than my voice.

Duffy retreated, jamming his fingers under the black claws cutting into his neck, all the time gasping for enough air to remain conscious.

"Fuck with Lucifer and you will die!"

I was watching the man I loved being killed by my own hands.

Duffy rolled his head and tore one of the clawed hands free from his throat. Then leveraging his own hand against the beast, he spun me around into the wall. The move surprised the demon and broke the diabolic grip of the second bony claw. But it accomplished little else.

"Trish!" he yelled.

I no longer heard. Something else, now laughing hideously, dominated what was my body and my mind.

Scaly cracked lips peeled back to expose jagged carious teeth.

"Come to Hell with me!" it said.

Duffy used that precious speck of a moment to think. His torch had fallen to the floor, and now sputtered at the edge of a puddle. When the creature whipped its arm around trying to snare Duffy's neck anew, Duffy ducked and came up with staff twirling.

The demon spat a stream of brown mush at him. It missed and splattered against the wall.

The demon skull's outline bulged through the pellucid skin tightened grotesquely across it. The green slits shot angry daggers at Duffy.

The flickering torchlight glinted off the Bloodstone I wore around my now constricted neck.

Duffy slammed the end of the staff into my gut as the diabolic hand gouged at his eye. The blow caused the claw to land low, knifing deep into his cheek and sending blood streaming down his chin.

The now vehement creature backhanded Duffy, cracking his jaw with a force far greater than human.

Duffy reeled around and swung the broom handle at the creature that now only resembled me in size and frame. It wrenched the stick from Duffy's grip, laughing.

"I'm going to rip off your cock and force it down your fucking throat," it said, charging.

Duffy grabbed wildly for the creature's neck, lost his tenuous hold and felt his feet slip on the slime. But as he dropped, he slipped a finger around the Bloodstone necklace.

The virile amulet dropped from around my neck.

In that instant, the beast issued an angry dying lament and recoiled against the wall.

Duffy pulled himself erect, regained his staff and lurched toward the form.

"Duffy, no!" I screamed, cowering in the darkness with my hands covering my face.

In that moment the demon had been forced to flee. The window to my soul opened by the Bloodstone had been closed. The flesh had to be surrendered. My soft blue eyes caught the torch-light, as peaceful now as a quiet stream.

I slumped down the wall, my energy spent by the demon who had inhabited my soul.

Duffy crushed the Bloodstone under foot and scrambled to catch me before I fell.

Inside the mock church, the worshippers stood spellbound and confused. But Asmodeus was not yet ready to leave this place. He had waited too long for this.

Kevel began to wail with his head arched back in lupine fashion.

"Give me the whoring bitch!" it screamed over the chaos.

"We've got to get Ali," Duffy commanded, shaking me to revitalize me. "Listen to me."

I stared at him vacantly for a long moment.

"We're going in there. Now! You go straight for Ali. Nothing else. No matter what happens. You hear me? You do nothing but get Ali. I'll take care of them. Get Ali and get out of here. If I don't follow you, get to the staircase and don't look back."

Duffy had run out of time to bark instructions. The door opened and a robed hulk filled the doorway.

****

Duffy's hands delivered the sting and fury of lightning bolts. Before his first assailant could fully withdraw his heavily ornate knife, used in their ceremonies, from beneath his robe, Duffy had him writhing in agony on the ground. A wretched scream wailed from inside that desecration of a church.

"Get them!" Kevel screeched from his station at the altar.

"Go!" Duffy commanded me.

Instead of retreating, Duffy launched a vicious attack on the worshippers in the room. Chaos reined. With staff and flying legs, Duffy knocked down the first two who rushed him. A swift round house kick kept the first to fall from getting back up. Another robed proselyte joined the melee.

I skirted the confrontation, saw with a quick side glance that Duffy was taking on the cult members as I made my way to Ali, who now stood dazed at the side of the altar.

Kevel spotted me, knew my intent, but mired down with indecision, failed to launch an attack. His mind like mine previously, must have been disoriented, being so abruptly returned to him from the demon.

I reached a hand out to a teetering Ali, whose eyes stared through me as if she had been disassociated from reality. There was no time to embrace. But behind that empty gaze, I saw glimmers of recognition. The sign of someone who realized she had just been pulled from the jaws of Hell.

I said nothing. Twenty feet away knife–wielding cult members were trying to surround Duffy.

"Hurry Trish!" he yelled.

Duffy whirled his staff in a wide arc, whacking a priest's head who lunged for him.

"Stop them!" Kevel screamed in a torrent, toppling the still kneeling nun at his side.

An arm grabbed my shoulder, arresting my flight. I swung a fist around.

Catwoman snarled at me, a crippled deformed hand clamping down and digging into my flesh.

"Leave the whoring bitch for us!" the grating voice demanded. The command issued from deep in Catwoman's throat.

"Fuck you!" I screamed, driving a second fist into Catwoman's jaw.

The claw released me. I drew Ali in close and together we started for the doors. I now had to hope Duffy could clear a path for our escape.

Kevel saw his precious prize in freedom's flight. He knew he must prevent our escape. It would mean his demise. His very life. He stretched for a burning candle.

I pulled Ali along, the doors inching closer.

With both of us beyond his reach, and fearing we might somehow bypass the foray at the doors, Kevel leapt from the altar and launched the candle like a grenade.

It needn't hit its target. Like a real grenade, close counted. The flame remained lit and the candle struck Ali in the back, hitting the ground at her feet. Her robe caught fire from a splatter of burning wax and the candle continued to roll beneath ragged draperies hanging on a side wall.

I screamed.

Duffy, too busy fending off the clan closing in like a pack of ferine animals, called for me to extinguish the flame.

I swung Ali around, smothering the flame by pressing my body against hers. It took a precious second, but the fire was gone.

Not so for the curtains. They roared into a hissing wall of blue and yellow fire. In seconds, flames licked the ceiling timbers. Thick choking smoke began to wash down from above.

"Let the bitches burn," Catwoman taunted, struggling back to her feet.

"Kill the bitches!" Kevel yelled, with gasps of desperation. He withdrew a gleaming curved-blade knife from beneath his saliva-coated vestments. In English he called upon his god Asmodeus to come to his aide.

Duffy focused mind and body totally on his enemies, relying on wing chun to keep the knife-wielding men at bay. He had to concentrate. If he faltered, even for a moment to look at me, one of them might slip a blade through.

Whatever that creature was he had faced earlier, in the eyes of his attackers, he saw no more demons. They were all now mere men.

Two fallen worshippers regained their footing, and now moved to block the doors—the only exit to this place filling with smoke and flames.

My scream alerted Duffy to the danger. It also awakened Ali from the nightmare controlling her mind.

Duffy flung a bench at an onrushing Kevel, kicked a priest in the jaw after averting his clumsy dagger thrust, then retreated to clear an escape path for us.

Feinting left, then launching a spinning kick to the right, Duffy toppled one of the two gate keepers. As he landed his blow, the second's dagger slit his forearm. Duffy disarmed the assailant by snapping the bone in the robed arm. He then positioned himself so we could slip through into the corridor.

Angry smoke curls spewed down into the hall. But the knee–level air remained clear and breathable. Flames spit through the timbers, threatening the cross corridor less than ten paces from our exit.

Duffy risked a second's pause to slide the staff through the handles, jamming the doors. It gave us a precious moment to flee.

But a second later, a torrent of bodies crashed through, pouring into the hall amid a rush of smoke.

****

Duffy, Ali and I ducked into a room on the first perpendicular corridor we came to. Smoke cascaded down the hallway, and so did the now panicking cult members.

Duffy applied pressure to stanch his bleeding arm, knowing we could never successfully fight our way through to the staircase.

"We have to get out of here!" I said.

"Listen."

A ringing bell one floor up.

"Fire alarm's tripped."

"We have to get to the stairs."

"No, Trish," Duffy said, still holding his arm. "You're cut."

"It's not bad. But I can't take on that many. I can't be sure I can get you and Ali out."

"So what do we do?"

Our lives were now being measured in seconds. The flames spread furiously over the aged timber supports. We had minutes left. If we went for the stairs, we would have to face Kevel and Simon.

"Those crates. Duffy, they're too large to have come down the staircase. How did they get them down here?" I said.

"You're right. There's got to be a loading ramp somewhere. That's the way out."

"Think Duffy. Where was it on the building plans."

Ali began to sob, pawing at me.

"Hold on, Ali. Please hold on. Think, Duffy!"

"Follow me."

Duffy led us back into the corridor. We crouched close to the floor; the smoke owned the space overhead.

Duffy turned down one lightless corridor, then, realizing his direction was in error, lead us the opposite way.

We came upon a set of doors with the handles missing, one slightly ajar.

"I hope I'm right. If it isn't..."

I wasted no time in deliberation. I kicked the door and plunged into the darkness.

The floor inclined with each step.

Duffy howled success. At the end of the ramp, we could see the pale studs of the wall addition to the basement level. The ringing bell grew louder.

Duffy felt around blindly. His hand found a length of rusted pipe. He banged it into the plaster. It went through with ease. Fresh, sweet air poured in through the long slit.

"Break down the frigging wall!" Duffy commanded me.

I screamed!

Kevel and Simon emerged out of the smoke billowing into the open area.

Duffy handed the pipe to me.

"Open that wall! Don't stop for anything."

Duffy positioned himself between us and Kevel. He saw their knives and blocked out the ripping pain in his arm. They had no intention of allowing Ali and me to escape. In their eyes, Duffy must have detected hesitation, for he attacked.

They knew Duffy intended to stop them.

My first hammers into the wall sent plaster flying across the basement floor.

"Trish," I heard Quenby yell from somewhere nearby. He had figured out the mystery behind the stone.

"We're here! Break down this wall! Hurry!"

Quenby grabbed a fire hose on the wall, pulled it until it would stretch no further, then began pounding the brass nozzle into the plaster. His meager hole started a few feet from where my pipe had struck through. With each new penetration, breathable air rushed in to surround us. Vital air that kept us alive. But air that also fanned the flames.

Duffy launched a furious flying assault, kicking the knife from Simon's hand. When he landed, Kevel slashed him in the thigh. Duffy made no sound, swinging a backhand that caught Kevel's head.

Kevel reeled backward, stopping inches from the creeping flames.

"Get out!" Duffy commanded, no longer sure he could keep the two at bay.

Quenby ripped away a stud, enlarging the hole enough for Ali's head to come through.

Wasting no time, Quenby grabbed an arm and pulled.

Ali slithered onto the basement floor. Smoke rolled in behind her.

I whirled around. I had one thing to do before going through.

The intense heat made breathing almost impossible. But I refused to abandon Duffy.

Simon lunged with his blade out. Duffy blocked the thrust with his good arm, backhanded Simon with his bad. The blow sent Simon reeling back into a lunging Kevel.

Simon's eyes bulged in anguish. He gasped as blood chortled from his mouth. Then he fell with a horrible looseness, like his bones had turned to jelly.

Kevel withdrew his knife from Simon's back.

An agonizing scream, that Duffy could no longer restrain, poured from his throat. The intense pain jarred his tenuous concentration.

I rushed forward in time to swing the rusted pipe in between Duffy and a charging Kevel. It was enough for Duffy to turn his body and grab the hand with the knife. He slammed it against his knee until the blade fell. When Kevel turned, Duffy's fist cracked his jaw. Kevel toppled backward, disappearing into the wall of smoke.

The flames crept along the ceiling, seeking the oxygenated air.

I stuck my head through the hole and into Quenby's waiting arms. As soon as my feet were through, Duffy's head, choking from the smoke, pushed out.

Quenby yanked Duffy through with one hand, assisted me to my feet with the other.

"This whole place is going up!" Quenby yelled over the roar of flames.

Quenby wrapped an arm around Ali's waist and pulled her up the stairs. Duffy and I, coughing and gasping, moved in unison right behind. At the top of the stairs we saw the EXIT sign for the side doors. Smoke folded into our wake.

Quenby froze. I stopped behind him.

"Freeze!" a voice yelled.

Merrifield stood with a shooter's stance, his gun leveled on the four of us. His eyes never strayed.

Duffy came up behind me.

"It's over!" Duffy yelled.

Merrifield fired.

The shot rang past Quenby and Ali, me and Duffy. It struck Kevel in the head. The knife he had lofted to arm's length, and poised to deliver into Duffy, glinted in the gun's flash.

"Now it's over," Merrifield said. He dropped his gun and stood there.

Quenby and Ali were the first to explode out the side doors, where red lights danced across the building. Firefighters rushed back and forth, barking commands. Hoses criss–crossed the ground as they battled the blaze roaring out of control.

The historic edifice was, by this time, totally engulfed.

A moment later Duffy and I punched through the smoke, huddled together. I held Duffy up, pulling him along while blood seeped down his arm and leg.

Paramedics rushed up to carry us to safety.

Doubled over at the rear of an ambulance, I coughed hard to eject smoke from my lungs. My throat burned every time I inhaled. I never realized how sweet fresh air could be.

"Damnit, I'm not one of them," I heard Quenby yelling as a policeman pulled him along in cuffs. "I went into that building to help Trish. I'm not one of them. I knew that was the only place where they would find a cave... It's the feast of Michaelmas, Crowley said..."

"It's all right. He saved us officer," I called out despite the fire that accompanied every word.

"Let him go. If she says he's all right. Then he's all right."

I knew that voice. When I looked up, Nick Logan stared down at me. He saw a peace in my blue eyes. I saw something in his eyes. Something I could never find words to explain. It was like he had found his own lost daughter.

"You did one hell of a job. This must be Althea Goodfellow."

Ali sat at arm's length, crying tears of joy, hunched over while one paramedic treated the burns on her arms and another started an IV. She looked emaciated and devoid of spirit. But she was alive!

"Jack, round them up and find the one named Kevel," Nick barked.

Ali was safe; a smile took over Nick's face. It was truly over.

I was speechless; tears stole away my vision. I slid one arm around Ali, reached out with the other.

Duffy's hand was there.

I held on to it with all my might.

"Good work, MacDuff, but you've made a mess of your arm. I guess now you're gonna expect medical leave?" Nick said. They exchanged a professional smile and a hand to Duffy's shoulder seemed all the recognition Duffy needed.

A string of police cars took over the walkway beside the building. On Nick's orders, county officers handcuffed Merrifield and the four youths who had emerged out the front doors of Chandler Hall.

"You know, I never got a chance back there to tell you something," Duffy said, drawing me under his good arm, covering me with his blanket.

"What's that?"

"I love you."

Epilogue

Three students died in the Chandler Hall blaze. More correctly, firefighters recovered three bodies from the charred remains of the old dead edifice. Catwoman's body, however, never turned up, and since she's never been seen around campus after that night, most believe she, too, perished. At times I wonder. The Administration blamed the entire incident on reckless, irresponsible student behavior beyond the control of all reasonable efforts by Ranhurst authorities. Reasonable efforts. Like there were ever reasonable efforts on their part to find Ali. Only a handful know the truth about what really happened that night of the coincident fulgent moon and lunar eclipse in September.

Ali never really learned why she was kidnapped that first night she returned to campus. Matt Evans had set her up, Ali confirmed that much. Was she to be sold to the Columbian druglords? Or sacrificed in the Satanic ritual? Those who knew the answer to these questions were certainly dead.

Nick Logan wasted no time closing his case. He confirmed, using the photograph I saw in Matt's room, that Kevel had indeed attended the University of Oregon during the time of one girl's disappearance. He was convinced that Kevel Moreland was the ringleader of the flesh trafficking to Colombia. Did he have any solid evidence beyond photo identification? If he did, he never revealed it to me, and Duffy was never solidly convinced. The number of young women in the 16 to 20 year old bracket reported missing each year in this country staggers the mind. We can only hope they are not falling victims to such a heinous crime.

Quenby and I still talk on occasion. Each time I hear his voice I am taken back to that night. He truly did save all our lives. And there really is no way to repay a deed of such courage. He believes to this day that Ali was meant to be a blood sacrifice to the demon Asmodeus. Though, he stands on his conviction that the whole belief system is preposterous. He has no idea how wrong he actually is. Later, many days after that terrible ordeal, I asked him why he went to Chandler Hall that night looking for me. If he hadn't broken into the building and battered down that wall, we would have perished. He called it a hunch after making the connection between the cave and blueprint.

I never revealed to another soul what I went through in that subbasement that night. At times I awake in an icy sweat, terrified, without knowing why. Elusive images from that horrible place still haunt me, and there are instances when I think voices remain from that night. Three months ago I received the Catholic sacrament of Holy Communion, and now I'm studying to be confirmed.

Ali Goodfellow eventually made the Olympic track team, but an ankle injury negated her chances of competing in Atlanta. I guess she's living proof you can't destroy the human spirit. I know in my heart she would have taken the gold had she made it there. She survived Ranhurst— she can achieve anything.

We heard later, months after I had left Ranhurst, that Merrifield's lawyer got him off without even a trial. Seems no one could prove Merrifield's connection to Kevel or the Delta Rho fraternity. I needed no more convincing than what I had seen and heard those three weeks I spent trying to locate Ali. Mine and Duffy's statements of that night provided ample proof that Merrifield fired to save Duffy from Kevel's knife. Merrifield professed to be the hero, all the while refusing to explain why he went to Chandler Hall that night with his gun.

And that leaves Duffy. It took me almost six months to be convinced that he really loved me. I think I knew for certain when he transferred from the San Francisco office to the Chicago office of the Drug Enforcement Agency then asked me to marry him. By the way, he became

Catholic shortly after me, and we're planning a spring wedding at Holy Name Cathedral in Chicago, where we attend mass faithfully every Sunday. I'm still pursuing my dream of becoming an FBI agent. Maybe I can make a difference.

Clausula.